THE
FIRST
AMENDMENT
UNDER SIEGE

THE
FIRST
AMENDMENT
UNDER SIEGE
THE POLITICS
OF BROADCAST
REGULATION

RICHARD E. LABUNSKI

Contributions in Political Science, Number 62

GREENWOOD PRESS
WESTPORT, CONNECTICUT • LONDON, ENGLAND

Library of Congress Cataloging in Publication Data

Labunski, Richard E
  The first amendment under siege.

  (Contributions in political science ; no. 62 ISSN
0147-1066)
    Bibliography: p.
    Includes index.
    1.   Broadcasting—Law and legislation—United States.
I. Title.   II. Series.
KF2805.L3   343.73'09945   80-39675
ISBN 0-313-22756-X

Library of Congress Catalog Card Number: 80-39675
ISBN: 0-313-22756-X
ISSN: 0147-1066

First published in 1981

Greenwood Press
A division of Congressional Information Service, Inc.
88 Post Road West
Westport, Connecticut 06881

Printed in the United States of America

10 9 8 7 6 5 4 3 2 1

This book is gratefully dedicated to those special people without whose emotional and financial support it would never have been written.

Contents

Foreword

So far as the First Amendment is concerned, the electronic media are neither fish nor fowl. Their claims to full First Amendment protection have been defeated by their status as enterprises licensed by the government to operate on condition that it is in the public interest, convenience, and necessity. In this important book, Richard Labunski analyzes the constitutional situation of the media in light of their "second-rate" First Amendment status and the consequences of this status for the industry and the public it entertains and enlightens.

No one who treasures the First Amendment and understands its role in a free society finds it easy, however, to accept the idea of its second-rate status as it affects agencies of communication that have become the most important channels for information about public affairs. In two valuable chapters of this book, the author covers sixty years of litigation as the media have resisted legislative or administrative action impinging on their autonomy. They have usually lost, in spite of the provision in the Federal Communications Act forbidding "censorship" of program content by the Federal Communications Commission (FCC). For example, in one of the most recent controversies, the Supreme Court, dividing five to four, held that FCC action against the use of "indecent language" on the air was not censorship and did not violate the First Amendment.

This book is more than a history of litigation, however. The author is a political scientist, and as the subtitle indicates, he is concerned broadly with the politics of broadcast regulation. He examines in some detail the "political environment" of the FCC—the selection process by which commissioners are chosen and their characteristics and the relationships among the FCC and the White House, Congress, the industry, and citizen groups.

Labunski is also a working broadcast journalist with ten years of news experience in radio and television. He brings to this study not only an academic background, but firsthand knowledge of the technical and commercial needs of the broadcast media.

A major political concern has been to assure against abuse of the quasi-monopoly powers that the media enjoy by reason of public grant. This concern has been implemented by the FCC "fairness doctrine" and guarantee of the right to respond to personal attacks, plus the congressional statute providing for equal time for political candidates. The fairness doctrine, upheld by the Supreme Court in the *Red Lion* case, is generally approved by the author, but he criticizes its abuse by the FCC in the NBC pensions program incident.

There is a certain irony in the fact that government regulation of broadcasting was justified initially because of the limited number of broadcast channels, whereas anyone could start a newspaper. Yet today in the United States, there are some 10,000 radio and television stations and only 2,000 daily newspapers. Technical developments may soon permit a great number of additional channels, and this fact plus the current interest in industrial deregulation may modify the current regulatory situation. But the author concludes that for the near future, at least, a constitutional distinction will continue to be drawn between the print and the electronic media.

C. HERMAN PRITCHETT

Introduction

The special position that the First Amendment is granted in our system is a recognition of the paramount importance of the free exchange of ideas to self-government. Freedom of speech and press provisions of the First Amendment are designed to prevent interference with the exchange of information if citizens are to make intelligent decisions when choosing public officials and shaping policy.

To an increasing degree, the American people receive that information from electronic media. Between 60 and 70 percent now claim that television is their primary source of news. But unlike newspapers and other print media, the broadcasting industry has been subject, almost from birth, to federal regulation. The central question becomes the extent to which the First Amendment permits the regulation of broadcasting.

Regulation is justified because the number of frequencies available in the broadcasting spectrum is limited. Theoretically, anyone with a printing press can print and distribute a newspaper, magazine, or handbill, but not everyone who wants to broadcast is able to do so. While limited access to broadcasting facilities justified regulation as the industry developed, some now argue that current technology allows substantially greater access to broadcasting and that constitutional distinctions between print and electronic media are inappropriate and damaging to the First Amendment.

Almost no one argues that broadcasting should be totally unregulated. But contemporary debate centers on whether the federal government should be involved in matters other than the technical aspects of broadcasting, particularly decisions that affect programming and news content. Simply put, should the government regulate the medium of communication by which its citizens learn what their government is doing? Such regulatory policies as the fairness doctrine, personal attack rules, equal opportunity doctrine, and other rules raise the most serious First Amendment questions.

This study examines the major issues raised by federal regulation of electronic communication and the environment in which that regulation takes place. Chapter 1 considers whether the decline of newspapers and the development of broadcasting have made the scarcity argument obsolete. In other words, is it damaging to First Amendment principles to continue to maintain that electronic and print media are not constitutionally parallel? Chapters 2 and 3 examine the development of case law in broadcasting and discuss the evolution of broadcasters' First Amendment rights. Chapter 4 considers the political environment in which broadcast regulation takes place, examining the Federal Communications Commission and its relationship with Congress, the White House, its clientele groups, and the public. Chapter 5 discusses First Amendment concepts of public interest, diversity, and access as they apply to the regulation of broadcasting. It is to promote those principles that such rules as the fairness doctrine are directed. Chapter 6 considers the current "rewrite" of the Communications Act of 1934 that is before Congress and discusses the consequences of changing the "public interest, convenience, and necessity" standard that has governed the regulation of broadcasting for fifty years. And the appendix provides an analytical model for evaluating the relative contributions of various actors to FCC policymaking and suggests issue areas for testing the model analytically.

At times this study may seem insensitive to the technical and commercial needs of broadcasters, particularly below the network level. However, broadcasters' overall lack of diligence in protecting and promoting their fragile First Amendment rights may have contributed to the environment that allows vigorous regulation of the industry. From the point of view of an insider, greater commitment to providing informative programming may be required without seriously affecting profits and without irreparably harming the First Amendment.

1.

A Constitutional Distinction Between Print and Electronic Media: Is It Obsolete?

An American family sitting in its living room in the 1920s could look forward to a wide selection of programs on its radio receiver. Unfortunately, programs were often broadcast over the same frequency. Listeners spent many frustrating hours deciphering one program from another. Until the late 1920s, the broadcasting industry was in a state of chaos, and the public and the broadcasters made incessant demands for government regulation.

Despite the existence of the Radio Act of 1912,[1] radio emerged in the 1920s almost totally unregulated. Nearly everyone who applied for a license could get one.[2] Whatever regulatory authority the Secretary of Commerce and Labor had been granted under the Radio Act was emasculated in 1923, when the District of Columbia Circuit Court held that the Secretary had no discretion to refuse a license to a radio applicant within certain classifications.[3] By 1926, the same court had all but eliminated the Secretary's power to direct the development of radio when it held that he could not penalize the Zenith Radio Corporation for broadcasting on an unauthorized frequency.[4]

There was great danger that with uncontrolled growth the new radio industry would become an arena of private interests competing for audiences by trying to outpower and outshout each other. Every one of the ninety channels in the broadcasting band was occupied by at least two stations, many by three or more. In urban areas, stations were forced to set up complicated time-sharing arrangements but would then deviate from the agreements. Established stations jumped from wavelength to wavelength and changed their wattage and operating hours at will.

Simply put, the broadcasting spectrum did not have enough space for all the stations to operate. Broadcasters and listeners barraged the federal government with complaints and demands for regulation. After Secretary of Commerce Herbert Hoover convened a series of radio conferences in the mid-1920s, Congress finally passed the first comprehensive broadcasting regulation bill, the Federal Radio Act of 1927.[5]

The Act created the Federal Radio Commission (FRC), an administrative agency charged with regulating and controlling traffic and with seeing that broadcasting was carried out according to the "public interest, convenience, or necessity."

The most important feature of the Act was that it established national policy for the regulation of radio that made the public interest "paramount" and that provided that broadcasting stations be operated by private individuals charged with the responsibility of serving the public interest. The airwaves were considered a public resource, not private property.[6]

The Federal Radio Commission was composed of five members with authority to grant, renew, or revoke station licenses. The Act provided that after one year all authority was to be vested in the Secretary of Commerce except that he would not have the authority to revoke a license and would be required to refer to the Commission all applications for controversial licenses, renewals, or modifications. The FRC was little more than an appeals board.

The authority provided in the Act never became vested in the Secretary of Commerce. Congress extended the one-year limitation, and the FRC continued to function as originally provided until Congress passed the Communications Act of 1934, when all authority to regulate radio was vested in the Federal Communications Commission.

The Federal Radio Act, while establishing some important principles, served primarily as interim machinery until the more permanent FCC was established. Among the most important of those principles was that a license did not give a broadcaster legal ownership rights to the frequency.

Significantly, from the birth of the industry, broadcasters themselves were intimately involved with the government agencies responsible for their regulation. Broadcast regulation was shaped at radio conferences that were convened for and largely run by broadcasters.

At the first radio conference, in 1922, Secretary Hoover stressed a theme that was to justify future regulation of the electronic media. He spoke of the need to eliminate radio interference in order to protect a natural resource. Hoover said that some government control was necessary to establish a "public right over the ether roads" so that "there may be no national regret that we have parted with a great national asset into uncontrolled hands."[7]

Almost no one would argue that broadcasting should be totally unregulated. The chaos of the 1920s showed that decisions concerning the allocation of frequencies, hours of operation, wattage, and other technical issues could not be left to broadcasters. Government regulation of the technical aspects of broadcasting was necessary if the industry was to develop.

Contemporary debate centers on two issues: whether the federal government should be involved in matters other than technical issues, including decision making that affects programming and news content; and whether conditions have changed sufficiently since the 1920s to warrant a reexamination of the relationship of broadcasting to those who regulate it. Because the initial justification for government regulation was the fixed number of broadcasting frequencies, it is important to consider if conditions in the 1920s fit the 1980s.

Such an examination requires an understanding that the print media have never been so regulated as has the broadcasting industry. Theoretically, no limit exists in terms of the number of newspapers, handbills, or periodicals that can be distributed, and government involvement has been limited by the First Amendment to the business practices of newspapers and to libel with some exceptions. The government has been unsuccessful in its attempts to force newspapers to serve the public interest.

Broadcasters constantly face such pressures.

Despite a tremendous amount of data, or because of them, it is difficult to determine whether conditions have changed to the extent that "scarcity" no longer accurately describes the availability of broadcasting channels and no longer justifies government regulation.

The broadcasting industry, according to some data, continues to grow, while the newspaper business continues to fall on hard times. Other data suggest, however, that newspapers will never be replaced by broadcast news and that newspapers will always be needed.

Listeners and viewers in most of the United States have many radio and television stations from which to choose.[8] At the end of 1980, 9,007 radio stations were operating in the United States: 4,599 were commercial AMs, 3,312 were commercial FMs, and 1,096 were noncommercial FMs. At the same time, 1,025 television stations were operating: 520 were commercial VHFs (very high frequency) and 237 were commercial UHFs (ultra high frequency); 106 were noncommercial VHFs and 162 were noncommercial UHFs. More than 77 million homes, or 98 percent of all homes, had television sets, and about 49 percent had more than one set. Technological development has not ended. Cable television provides the potential for a much greater number of spaces in the television band, and within the decade, the more than 3,000 existing cable systems may be joined by some 5,000 more.[9] In addition, hundreds of "low power" television stations may be on the air within a few years.

While broadcasting has flourished, there are indications that newspaper readership has dropped. At the end of 1974, there were only 1,768 daily newspapers in the United States, slightly above the all-time low.[10] But the decline in readership is greater than statistics show. During the past two decades, when television has become the primary source of news for most Americans, the per capita circulation of newspapers has plummeted. According to census data, newspaper circulation in 1950 was 1.24 papers per household. It dropped to 1.12 papers by 1960 and to 0.99 papers by 1970 and is still dropping.[11] Most Americans who read newspapers today read no more than one paper, and many do not read any paper at all.

Another way to examine the decline of newspapers is through daily sales. From 1973 to 1975, the number of daily newspapers sold in the United States dropped 4.6 percent, and the number of people who read a daily newspaper dropped more than 7 percent. This is the first such decline in more than forty years.[12]

Perhaps even more significant to a reexamination of broadcast regulation is the fact that 97.5 percent of the daily newspapers in this country have no in-town competition. Fewer than fifty American cities have competing daily newspapers.[13]

The independence of newspapers has also diminished. In 1930, only 16 percent of American daily newspapers, with 43 percent of total daily circulation, were part of a chain. By 1960, 30 percent of all dailies, with 46 percent of circulation, had been bought by chains. Today, 60 percent of all dailies, with 71 percent of circulation, are controlled by chains.[14]

Even worse, writes journalist Tom Wicker, is that 52 percent of national newspaper circulation is supplied by the twenty-five largest chains, and the bigger chains are beginning to swallow the smaller ones.[15]

Many American cities have lost newspapers in recent years, while the number of radio and television stations has increased. Since 1960, daily newspapers have gone out of business in New York, Chicago, Los Angeles, Boston, San Francisco, Detroit, Houston, and Cleveland.[16] It is not unusual for a major city to have only one or two daily newspapers but many radio and television stations. Before its long newspaper strike of 1963, New York had twelve dailies. Today, three daily papers but almost one hundred radio and television stations serve the New York metropolitan area. San Francisco and Los Angeles each have two daily newspapers but are served by many radio and television stations.[17]

Although it is not within the scope of this study to examine American newspapers, David Shaw's comments are telling:

Unfortunately, some papers have . . . resorted to short-term circulation builders that many think will prove counterproductive— games and sweepstakes, front-page gossip columns, daily soap operas, a sensationalistic, yellow-journalism approach to the news. Even the historically staid *New York Times*—down 112,000 readers from 1970 to 1975—joined the circulation war this year, sponsoring and promoting a search for the Loch Ness Monster.[18]

Ironically, the success of television news has caused print journalism to assume some of the most undesirable characteristics of broadcast news. While newspapers are still primarily interested in "journalism," they have been tempted to give readers what they want instead of what they need.

The decline of newspapers and the increase in the number of American cities with no in-town newspaper competition have ramifications far beyond simple sentimentality. The key issue is diversity of viewpoints, the notion of a marketplace of ideas.

The First Amendment is granted a special position in our system in recognition of the importance of the free exchange of ideas to self-government. As Judge Learned Hand observed:

Right conclusions are more likely to be gathered out of a multitude of tongues, than through any kind of authoritarian selection. To many this is, and always will be folly; but we have staked upon it our all.[19]

The First Amendment prevents the government from interfering with the exchange of ideas and information necessary for a citizen to make intelligent decisions about government. But the restraint that competitive forces in the commercial marketplace put on the debate of public issues is as serious as government interference.

Theoretically, the more avenues of communication, the more likely there will be diversity of viewpoints. If the same individuals or corporations control most or all forms of communication in an area, it does not matter if the information is delivered by print or by electronic media.

The only newspaper in town also will often own the only radio or television station in town. In recent years, the FCC has ordered some of the communications monopolies to break up. On June 12, 1978, the U.S. Supreme Court, in *Federal Communications Commission v. National Citizens Committee for Broadcasting*,[20] held that under the Communications Act the FCC can forbid the establishment of jointly owned newspaper-broadcast station combinations located within the same community and can require those "egregious" combinations that involve a community's sole daily newspaper or sole broadcasting station to be disbanded within five years. However, the Court found only sixteen such "egregious" cases and left the other cross-ownerships intact.

Although newspaper readership is apparently declining and the ownership of mass media is increasingly monopolized, a tremendous amount of information is, nevertheless, available to those who want it.

Today, for example, approximately 8,300 weekly newspapers and some 9,000 other periodicals are published in this country, including more than 150 magazines of general circulation; more than 280 million books are published each year, and nearly 200 motion pictures are released annually for general exhibition in more than 13,000 theaters.[21] In short, information is available to those who are interested.

Despite the various sources of information, television provides more and more of that information; surveys now indicate that between 60 and 70 percent of the American people rely on television as their primary source of news.[22] Moreover, trends indicate that in the decades ahead television will play an even more significant role in disseminating information. But for a number of reasons, the medium is not well-suited to providing serious, comprehensive coverage of complex public policy issues.

At the same time that television has grown, government regulation has intruded into programming and news content to a far greater degree than in earlier years when the allocation of frequencies and the hours of operation were the most pressing issues. Section 326 of the Communications Act protects broadcasters from censorship, but it has not always done so:

Nothing in this Act shall be understood or construed to give the Federal Communications Commission the power of censorship over the radio communications or signals transmitted by any radio station, and no regulation or conditions shall be promulgated or fixed by the Commission which shall interfere with the right of free speech by means of radio communications.[23]

Although this is not a history of the broadcasting industry in terms of federal regulation, it is vital to understand the mechanism of modern regulation.

At the outset, a general statement can be made about federal regulation of the broadcasting industry: Government involvement in matters other than the technical aspects of the industry has evolved steadily because of the nature of the political environment in which the industry is regulated and because broadcasters, themselves, content with substantial profits, have lacked diligence in pressing for full First Amendment rights.

Four basic regulatory policies affect what is seen and heard on television and radio: the equal opportunity requirement, the fairness doctrine, the personal attack rules, and the political editorial rules. As mentioned before, newspapers are not bound by such policies.

Some have argued that new technology has provided greater access to broadcasting facilities and that government regulation is no longer needed, except for controls that also affect print media. Broadcasters are subject to the same libel laws that apply to print journalists,[24] and some believe that these are the only intrusion into First Amendment rights our system of government can tolerate. In addition, the fairness doctrine and other regulations may actually inhibit broadcast coverage of controversial issues and cause timidity among those who rely on government licenses to stay in business.

Because they lie at the heart of any discussion of broadcasters' First Amendment rights, let us first discuss these four regulatory policies.

THE EQUAL OPPORTUNITY REQUIREMENT

The equal opportunity requirement has its roots in the Federal Radio Act of 1927 and was carried over to section 315 of the Communications Act of 1934.[25] The first part of the policy reads:

If any licensee shall permit any person who is a legally qualified candidate for any public office to use a broadcasting station, he shall afford equal opportunities to all other such candidates for that office in the use of such broadcasting station; provided, that such licensee shall have no power of censorship over the material broadcast under the provisions of this section. No obligation is imposed upon any licensee to allow the use of its station by any such candidate.[26]

In other words, broadcasters may either accept requests for time from all political candidates for the same office or accept none. Faced with that option, broadcasters have often preferred to avoid controversy and the loss of control over their stations by not accepting any such requests. This attitude, however, does not square with the broadcasters' responsibility to serve the public interest by providing a forum for political debate by candidates for public office. Moreover, it is particularly disappointing because this forum is among the most valuable contributions broadcasting can make.

In a series of rulings following enactment of the Communications Act, the FCC further explained what is meant by equal opportunity for candidates for public office. For example, the Commission determined that the candidate must receive not only as much time but also as desirable time. A half-hour on Sunday at 9 A.M. is not an equal opportunity for a candidate whose opponent had prime evening time.[27] This does not mean that all candidates must be given exactly the same opportunity, such as appearances on a regularly scheduled discussion program. But the Commission has required that licensees be "fair" to both sides.

Problems have arisen in the definition of legally qualified candidates specified in section 315. Generally, the Commission has considered eligible those who have announced that they are running for nomination or for election, those who can be voted for, and those who can serve if elected.

The equal opportunity requirement remains highly controversial and has been blamed for the lack of coverage of such important races as presidential elections. The problem of multiple candidacies continues to limit broadcasters' willingness to air appearances by the major-party presidential candidates. For the most part, debates and discussions of issues by those seeking the presidency have been limited. In 1960, section 315 was suspended to allow the Kennedy-Nixon debates; in 1976, the

Ford-Carter people convinced the League of Women Voters to stage a "debate" as a bona fide news event that side-stepped the problem of offering time to all other candidates. In the years ahead, deciding which candidates to include in debates will likely be even more complicated and controversial.

Broadcasters continue to complain that section 315 inhibits coverage of controversial issues during political campaigns despite the efforts of Congress to exempt certain types of programs from its requirements. In 1959, Congress amended section 315 to exempt a bona fide newscast, a bona fide news interview, a bona fide news documentary, and on-the-spot coverage of a bona fide news event.[28]

Problems continue to plague broadcasters, however. For example, the FCC has decided that a president's press conference is not exempt from section 315 because he, rather than the media, controls the format of the event, and it therefore cannot be considered a bona fide news interview. On the other hand, the Commission has decided that televising his report on an international crisis escapes the restriction because it is on-the-spot coverage of a bona fide news event.[29]

THE FAIRNESS DOCTRINE

In its present form, the fairness doctrine is the name given to two requirements imposed by the FCC on radio and television broadcasters. The first, known as the Part One requirement, demands that broadcast licensees devote a reasonable amount of their programming to controversial issues of public importance. The second part requires that when such issues are presented contrasting viewpoints must be aired.[30] Broadcasters are therefore charged by the Commission with an *affirmative* duty to seek out and to broadcast opposing or contrasting viewpoints on important, public issues.

In the words of the U.S. Supreme Court, the doctrine requires that "discussion of public issues be presented on broadcast stations, and that each side of those issues . . . be given fair coverage."[31]

Part Two of the fairness doctrine, the fairness-balancing part of the doctrine, is by far the better known of the two requirements and has a long history in broadcasting regulation, even going back to years before it was called a fairness doctrine.

Over the years, the vast majority of FCC cases dealing with the fairness doctrine have focused on Part Two complaints. Many observers feel that Part One has been seriously neglected by the Commission. In very few cases has the FCC ever ordered a radio or television station to cover an issue that it had been ignoring.[32] In terms of litigation, Part One dates only from the 1940s, while Part Two has a longer history.

For the most part, the two sections evolved from regulatory action on the part of the Federal Radio Commission and later the Federal Communications Commission. Subsequent congressional action in the 1950s appeared to codify what was already the practice: that broadcasters have a responsibility to present public issues and to do so fairly. In the opinion of the U.S. Supreme Court, Congress had "ratified" the fairness doctrine with positive legislation.[33] The Court also held that "when Congress ratified the FCC's notion of a 'fairness doctrine' in 1959 it did not, of course, approve every past decision or pronouncement by the Commission on this subject, or give it a completely free hand for the future. The statutory authority does not go so far."[34]

Whether the fairness doctrine is an instrument created by the FCC and approved by Congress or whether it was legislated by Congress in the 1959 Amendments is an issue with some relevance. If the doctrine was an FCC policy that Congress merely acknowledged, then presumably the Commission could change it without specific congressional approval. On the other hand, if Congress incorporated the doctrine's obligations into statute with the 1959 Amendments, then it could be changed only by Congress.

In either case, most observers agree that the requirements of the fairness doctrine were stated with sufficient clarity in the 1959 Amendments that changing its underlying principles would require congressional approval. If the Commission were to attempt unilateral changes, the courts and Congress would probably protest that it no longer had such authority.

The doctrine itself has been the source of much controversy. Because of what had been a scarcity of broadcasting channels, it was assumed that broadcasters had a legal responsibility to serve in the public interest. Such a responsibility is not shared by the print media.

Regardless of one's definition, serving the "public interest" involves the question of access. When broadcasting facilities are used for discussion of controversial issues of public importance, the radio or television station is compelled to cover those issues fairly. This obviously means that on some occasions "editorial" and content decisions are made by nonbroadcasters. The courts have prevented the government and others from interfering with editorial decisions by print journalists.[35]

The requirements under the doctrine are stated clearly in the FCC *Report on Editorializing* issued in 1949, ten years before congressional action on the document:

> The licensee, in applying the fairness doctrine, is called upon to make reasonable judgments in good faith on the facts of each situation—as to whether a controversial issue of public importance is involved, as to what viewpoints have been or should be presented, as to the format and spokesmen to present the viewpoints, and all the other facets of such programming.[36]

The Part One requirement, charging broadcasters with the responsibility of seeking out issues of public importance, has been the source of some controversy but has rarely been invoked by the Commission. It remains extremely rare for the Commission to instruct a licensee to cover a news story of importance to his community.[37]

The Part Two requirement has caused broadcasters many more problems. The 1959 Amendments exempted from equal time requirements but not from fairness responsibilities various kinds of programs, such as bona fide news programs and documentaries.

In deciding whether the issue raised in the initial broadcast is controversial and of public importance, and whether a reasonable opportunity to present differing views has been provided, the Commission defers, for the most part, to the licensee's judgment:

> The Commission does not seek to establish a rigid formula for compliance with the fairness doctrine. The mechanics of achieving fairness will necessarily vary with the circumstances, and it is within the discretion of each licensee, acting in good faith, to choose an appropriate method of implementing the policy to aid and encourage expression of contrasting viewpoints.[38]

While the Commission has left much discretion to the licensee and claims it does not issue specific rules on how to comply with Part Two requirements, it has in some decisions demonstrated a callous disregard for the journalistic function of broadcast news. Perhaps the clearest example of abuse of the fairness doctrine by the Commission was the case of *National Broadcasting Company v. Federal Communications Commission.*[39] Known as the Pensions case, the Commission concluded that an NBC documentary had violated the fairness doctrine and that the network must provide those with contrasting viewpoints an opportunity to respond. Despite the fact that the U.S. Court of Appeals for the District of Columbia later reversed the FCC decision,[40] it stands as one of the most blatant examples of Commission interference with programming decisions. The Pensions case will be discussed in chapter 3.

PERSONAL ATTACK AND POLITICAL EDITORIAL RULES

Somewhat less controversial than other sections of the fairness doctrine are the rules governing personal attacks and political editorials. Dating back several decades, the rules were formalized in 1967 and 1968. They state:

> When a broadcast attacks the integrity or character of a person or group, or an editorial supports or opposes a political candidate, the station must promptly notify the person attacked or opposed, furnish him with the content of the attack, and offer him air time to respond.[41]

It was the personal attack rule that the U.S. Supreme Court affirmed in the famous *Red Lion* decision, although the Court spoke in broad terms about the constitutionality of the fairness doctrine. Some believe that the facts in the *Red Lion* case ill-served the cause of broadcasters' asserting their First Amendment rights.[42] *Red Lion* was a case that would have been hard to decide any other way. An attack was made on the character and integrity of an individual by a radio station that refused to grant him any opportunity to respond. The Court felt that out of a sense of fairness he should have been afforded a right to defend himself. The Court's decision affirmed the constitutionality of the fairness doctrine itself.

The Commission has developed specific rules regarding a personal attack that require a broadcaster to notify the target of an attack promptly and to furnish him with a transcript, tape, or summary of the attack. He must also be given time to reply. Where the licensee has broadcast an editorial endorsing or opposing a political candidate, the opposing candidates are supposed to be notified within twenty-four hours after the broadcast and furnished with the transcript and an offer of time.[43]

As with section 315, certain types of programs are exempt from the provisions of the personal attack policy: a bona fide news event, news interviews, and commentaries made during a newscast. This leaves editorials and documentaries among the types of programs that remain under the special requirements.[44]

The Commission recognizes that the above requirements may discourage broadcasters from covering or airing important but controversial issues. Many radio and television stations have chosen not to endorse candidates rather than provide time for the other candidates to reply.

One problem raised by the personal attack rules also plagues victims of attacks by print media: many days or weeks may pass between the initial attack and the response, which may significantly lessen the impact of the response. For individuals attacked in the print media, the most appealing solution may be a libel suit, despite the cost and time necessary to see the case

through the courts. While individuals attacked on a radio or television station can sue for libel, some courts seem willing to limit damages if there was an offer of time to respond. In that case, the response may have little impact except to limit damages awarded to the plaintiff.[45] The FCC rarely fines or severely punishes stations for making personal attacks. While it has happened, it is most unlikely that a station will lose its license if it makes even a modest effort to provide time for response to a personal attack.[46]

For years, broadcasters have complained, as they did in the *Red Lion* case, that notifying the attacked individual in advance or promptly after the attack, sending tapes or transcripts, and offering time to respond are expensive and impose a burden on broadcasters that violates their First Amendment rights. They claim that the requirements inhibit or discourage coverage of controversial issues where there is the possibility of an attack on the personal character or integrity of an individual.

PROVOCATIVE PROGRAMMING

One final issue raised by FCC rules concerns so-called provocative programming. The Commission, until the last few years, appeared to be relatively tolerant of what some have called "alternative" programming, particularly on radio stations. In several cases involving stations owned by the Pacifica Foundation in the 1960s, the Commission ruled that listeners who were offended did not have the right to insist that the Commission deny the station its license. This attitude could perhaps be explained in part by the general permissiveness of the 1960s and by the composition of the Commission.

But in 1978, in the case of *Federal Communications Commission v. Pacifica Foundation,*[47] the U.S. Supreme Court held that the Commission was correct in ruling that a monologue by comedian George Carlin could not be aired on radio or television when there is a reasonable chance that children may be in the audience. The Commission acted after receiving one complaint from the father of a young boy who heard the Carlin monologue over Pacifica's WBAI-FM in New York City. While the

Commission did not penalize WBAI, it warned that the use of the "Seven Words You Can't Say on Television" could result in future action against a radio or television station. The Commission was reversed by a 2-1 decision in the U.S. Court of Appeals for the District of Columbia. The U.S. Supreme Court, reversing the Appeals Court, held that the Commission was correct in banning the words and was acting within its authority when it threatened to penalize stations that broadcast such programs in the future. The case will be discussed in chapter 3.

For the most part, this chapter has discussed some of the major issues concerning the basis of regulation of the broadcasting industry and the problems that broadcasters have had asserting their First Amendment rights. Another First Amendment issue of both theoretical and practical significance must be mentioned: the First Amendment rights of viewers and listeners to receive information that equips them to make intelligent decisions as citizens, particularly as voters.

According to democratic theory, a representative government serves best when those it serves are relatively well informed about what their government is doing. In our system of federalism, where elected and appointed officials at all levels make important policy decisions, it is crucial that citizens have access to accurate and widespread information about the decisions and activities of such public officials.

Analogous to this is the principle that lies at the heart of broadcast regulation: the concept of localism, which requires that, when granted a license, a broadcaster be judged on his ability to ascertain and serve the needs of his community. "Localism," however, is largely a myth. In most American cities, citizens learn relatively little about what their local public officials are doing by watching television or listening to the radio. They are more likely to see nightly coverage of fires, automobile accidents, raids on "porno" shops, demonstrations, and anything else that makes "exciting" news.

Moreover, the relationship between the local station and the network negates the concept of localism. Relatively little programming originates from the local station, and in many cities, local programming is almost unwatchable. While every television and radio station has a news "department" that spends some time "covering" local news, the quality of that coverage varies greatly. Often citizens cannot learn much about what is happening in their city unless they also read what is probably the only newspaper in town. Furthermore, the FCC has shown almost no inclination to monitor the quality of local news coverage, and no station has ever lost its license because it devoted too much time to fires and automobile accidents and stories provided by the wire services.

Still, a legitimate First Amendment right does entitle viewers and listeners to be provided information about their community in return for the granting of a valuable license. They have a First Amendment right to varied opinions so that as voters they can make the best choices. The broadcast media have a responsibility to help citizens "shop" in the marketplace of ideas. Along with the right of access to ideas goes a second, more complex issue: the right of access to broadcasting facilities. Some argue that viewers and listeners have a right to use broadcast facilities to promote discussion of their point of view, even though such facilities are privately owned. This argument raises serious questions and requires more in-depth examination.

This chapter has thus far failed to answer directly the question posed in its title: Is the constitutional distinction between print and electronic media obsolete? In other words, have conditions changed sufficiently since the birth of broadcasting to warrant a reexamination of the way the industry is regulated today? Or even if conditions have changed, should the regulatory policy that has evolved over the last half-century be discarded merely because the scarcity argument is less relevant?

Such questions are difficult to answer. Clearly, conditions have changed since the 1920s, and new technology provides the potential for much greater access to broadcasting facilities. In addition, many Americans today live in cities served by only one daily newspaper, but they can turn to a number of radio and television stations for information.

The broadcasting industry undoubtedly is among the most important in the country. Broadcasting stations do provide various forms of entertainment and information that are helpful to citizens. And despite the worst fears, television has not replaced books and newspapers, although certainly reading habits and life-styles have changed.

But does the existence of more radio and television stations and fewer newspapers suggest that broadcasting should be deregulated? An introductory answer would be that despite changes in the last fifty years newspapers and broadcasting stations are not identical. At the same time, it is dangerous to assume that since they are not constitutionally equal government ought to be intimately involved in programming and news decisions in order to "enforce" fairness and responsibility. As will be discussed later, such efforts can lead to government intimidation and harassment and can affect news coverage by inducing timidity and "self-censorship" on the part of broadcasters.

Print and broadcast journalists do not have identical First Amendment rights. Existing conditions still demand that a constitutional distinction be made between the two media. But the form of that distinction and the restrictions placed on the First Amendment rights of broadcasters remain to be discussed in greater detail. Broadcasters do suffer under a "second-rate" First Amendment, but the reasons are complex and deserve careful examination.

NOTES

1. 37 Stat. 199. Some students disagree as to whether the Wireless Ship Act of 1910 or the Radio Act of 1912 was the nation's first radio legislation. The 1910 Act had been concerned exclusively with the use of radio aboard ships at sea and provided no basis for regulating the explosive growth of radio in the 1920s. The incentive for the 1912 Act appeared to have been the sinking of the *Titanic* during the night of April 14—15, 1912. It was revealed later that rescue efforts were hampered when ship-to-shore radio communications were jammed by mainland radio signals. Steven J. Simmons, "Fairness Doctrine: The Early History," 29 *The Federal Communications Bar Journal* (1976): 15.

2. Walter B. Emery, *Broadcasting and Government: Responsibilities and Regulation* (East Lansing: Michigan State University Press, 1971), pp. 26-27.

3. Simmons, p. 215.

4. Ibid., p. 216.

5. 55 Stat. 1162.

6. Prior to the passage of the Communications Act, there had been pressure to establish a system of government ownership patterned after systems

adopted in other countries, but Congress rejected the idea. Emery, p. 39.

7. Simmons, p. 222.

8. Broadcasting Yearbook, 1980. Published yearly by *Broadcasting Magazine* (Washington, D.C.)

9. David L. Lange, "The Role of the Access Doctrine in the Regulation of the Mass Media: A Critical Review and Assessment," 52 *The North Carolina Law Review* (November 1973): 15.

In June 1980, a twenty-four-hour-a-day network devoted entirely to news went on the air. Connected by cable and satellite, Cable News Network could reach 2.2 million homes when it began operations. Its financial success and survival will depend on its ability to add more cable systems, and thus more television households, to its potential audience.

10. Lou Cannon, *Reporting: An Inside View* (Sacramento: California Journal Press, 1977), p. 79.

11. Ibid.

12. David Shaw, "Newspapers Challenged as Never Before," *Los Angeles Times* (November 26, 1976), p. 1.

13. Tom Wicker, *On Press* (New York: The Viking Press, 1978), p. 165.

14. Ibid.

15. Ibid.

16. Shaw, p. 1.

17. This refers to dailies *based* in the major cities. Suburban dailies obviously serve various parts of the metropolitan area.

18. Shaw, p. 26.

19. Roscoe L. Barrow, "The Fairness Doctrine: A Double Standard for Electronic and Print Media," 26 *The Hastings Law Journal* (January 1975): 663-64.

20. 76-1471.

21. Lange, p. 15. The 280 million books figure refers to press runs, not individual titles, but does indicate the public's appetite for books.

22. Roper Surveys, Survey conducted in November, 1980, reported 64% of respondents named t.v. as primary source of news. *Broadcasting Magazine* (April 13, 1981): 84.

23. The role of section 326 in litigation will be discussed in the next two chapters.

24. In *Rosenbloom v. Metromedia*, 403 U.S. 29 (1971), the Supreme Court did not distinguish between laws of libel and laws of slander.

25. Harold L. Nelson and Dwight L. Teeter, Jr., *Law of Mass Communications: Freedom and Control of Print and Broadcast Media* (Mineola, N.Y.: The Foundation Press, Inc., 1969), p. 411.

26. Ibid., p. 412.

27. Ibid.

28. Frank J. Kahn, *Documents of American Broadcasting*, 2d ed. (Englewood Cliffs, N.J.: Prentice-Hall, Inc., 1973), p. 80.

29. Nelson and Teeter, p. 415.

30. Simmons, pp. 207-08.

31. *Red Lion Broadcasting Company v. Federal Communications Commission,* 395 U.S. 367, 369 (1969).

32. The *Patsy Mink* case, a rare exception, will be discussed in chapter 6.

33. 395 U.S. at 381.

34. 395 U.S. at 385.

35. *Miami Herald Publishing Company v. Tornillo,* 418 U.S. 241 (1974).

36. Nelson and Teeter, p. 415.

37. See 59 F.C.C. 2d (1976).

38. Simmons, p. 209.

39. The case will be discussed in chapter 3.

40. 516 F.2d 1101 (1974).

41. Nelson and Teeter, p. 420.

42. Fred W. Friendly, *The Good Guys, the Bad Guys, and the First Amendment* (New York: Vintage Books, 1976), chapters 1-5.

43. Nelson and Teeter, p. 420.

44. Ibid.

45. Whether damages are limited by offers to respond depends on state libel laws, not federal policy. Some states provide for the limiting of punitive or special damages if a retraction or right-to-reply is offered by a newspaper, magazine, or other print media outlet.

46. In the few cases where the FCC has refused to renew licenses because of personal attack violations, the licensee had been guilty of other serious violations of FCC rules as well.

47. 77-528.

2.

The Courts and Broadcast Regulation: The Federal Radio Act to 1960

The Federal Communications Commission (FCC) was created in 1934 as an "independent" regulatory agency and was provided with institutional safeguards designed to insulate it from political pressures.[1] Just how independent and insulated the Commission is from various groups and individuals is the subject of much controversy. The FCC operates in a complex "political" environment. Numerous actors interact with the Commission and each other to form communications policy. Courts, Congress, the White House, executive agencies, broadcasters, and others are involved with various aspects of broadcast regulation. The judicial system requires separate examination. Despite the fact that the courts are part of the larger political system shaping communications policy and that there are no sets of issues with which the courts alone are concerned, it is important to consider the courts separately for several reasons.

First, the Federal Communications Commission regulates no ordinary industry. As media of communication, the broadcasting industry plays a vital role in disseminating information, and its regulation raises substantial constitutional questions. Without the informing function of mass media, citizens would be seriously hampered in their ability to make intelligent decisions. By the very nature of its jurisdiction, the Commission is intimately involved with the First Amendment and other basic constitutional issues. The Commission needs judicial guidance in interpreting the First Amendment.

Second, under the general guidance of the First Amendment and the Communications Act of 1934, the Commission is charged with the sensitive task of determining what constitutes the "public interest" and how it is to be served. Constitutional questions are inevitably raised when the Commission takes all but the most minor actions regarding the public interest doctrine. The FCC is forced to deal with numerous issues and cases, and it is faced with a formidable task when it applies the First Amendment, case law, and statutory language to those cases. The courts have been actively involved in guiding the Commission in making those decisions.

Third, the courts in the twentieth century[2] have been involved in defining the circumstances under which the First Amendment's freedom of speech and freedom of press clauses are applied. The courts' involvement in defining the First Amendment's relevance to broadcasting can be seen as part of a more active judiciary interested generally in civil liberties. In fact, much of the courts' activity in broadcasting cannot be isolated from their increasing activity in other policy areas.

Finally, the language of the Communications Act of 1934 does not define congressional intent for the regulation of broadcasting. The Act of 1934 would be described more accurately as a general legislative "charter" than as a clear statement of congressional conscience. Because the words "public interest, convenience, or necessity" have so little content in themselves, the regulatory agency is provided wide discretion to interpret those words and to determine what Congress would do on the many issues before the Commission.

In recent decades, judicial activity concerning programming content has increased. The Commission can no longer assume, if it ever did, that the courts will leave undisturbed complex and highly technical decisions. Although interested in communications issues since the birth of broadcasting, the courts' recent level of activity suggests that a "supervisory" relationship may exist between the courts and the Commission. Perhaps such a relationship is inevitable when a regulatory agency is involved with media of communication.

One court that has been particularly active in the regulation of broadcasting is the U.S. Court of Appeals for the District of Columbia (USCADC).[3] In some ways, this court can be described as a "super-Federal Communications Commission." It has not hesitated to involve itself in many complex and important issues dealing with broadcasting.

Most appeals from the FCC go to this Court of Appeals because it has statutory jurisdiction over license cases, the most numerous coming before the Commission. Also, most communications lawyers practice in Washington, and they find the D.C. Circuit convenient.

One court's intimate involvement in broadcasting cases has several consequences:

1. The USCADC has greater familiarity with issues concerning broadcasting and can be described as a tribunal "expert" on certain types of complex issues. Concentrating cases in that court not only increases its judges' knowledge, but also enhances their influence. It is probably accurate to suggest that judges who feel well informed are less likely to be "restrained" than are judges who feel that technical decisions should be left to a regulatory agency.

2. The court, apparently welcoming its activist role, has relatively liberal rules of standing. In numerous cases, it has allowed access to more "general" public interests.[4]

3. The scope of review of regulatory decisions is defined in the Administrative Procedure Act of 1946,[5] but its language is such that almost any decision by the Federal Communications Commission could be reviewed by an aggressive Court of Appeals. The absence of clear standards of review creates problems that will be considered below.

4. Although both federal judges and FCC commissioners are nominated by the President and are confirmed by the Senate, they are chosen for different reasons and are expected to perform different duties. FCC commissioners are appointed to seven-year terms, but fewer than half complete a full term.

Federal judges are appointed for life and serve for a significantly longer period of time than FCC commissioners. Life tenure, it is safe to conclude, gives the court much greater independence from the pressures of clientele groups, Congress, and others who exercise significant influence at the Commission. While tenure does not necessarily mean that outcomes of the decisions will be different, it does suggest that the USCADC may be the only "independent" agency overseeing the communications industry. As will be seen in chapter 4, the Commission, which was created and given its statutory authority by Congress, enjoys very close ties with the legislature and the regulated industries. The court enjoys much greater independence from Congress. While Congress does have some control over the jurisdiction, organization, and remedies of the lower federal courts, its relationship to the FCC is very different from its relationship to the courts.

5. Because the Court of Appeals reviews FCC decisions, the Commission is forced to "prove" its case and to explain its reasoning. Unlike a hearing before the Commission, an appeal before the court means that the FCC is a party and is therefore forced to convince a group of judges of the correctness and legality of its decisions. Forcing the Commission to explain itself may reveal pro-industry bias.

6. But it does appear that the FCC is better equipped than the courts to gain compliance with decisions. The Commission has many sanctions it can impose on broadcasters, ranging from fines to revocations of licenses. The courts, on the other hand, are limited in their ability to force compliance. On occasion, when the FCC has strenuously resisted clear instructions from the courts, it has taken a number of subsequent trips to the court before the Commission complied with the ruling.

BROADCASTING CASES

As with any discussion of judicial process, broad statements about the direction of judicial decisions are difficult to make. It is easier to trace judicial activism than judicial ideology. Nevertheless, by examining a number of cases, conclusions may be drawn about the role of courts in shaping regulatory policy.

This chapter and the next examine seventeen cases that deal with various aspects of communications policy. The cases are arranged chronologically, although this ordering should not lead to fixed conclusions about the direction of the courts at any particular time.

Since passage of the Federal Radio Act of 1927, the federal courts have ruled on literally hundreds of cases dealing with broadcasting. The cases discussed in these two chapters were chosen because a number of them review Commission decisions that in some way affect the content of programming. Such decisions by the Commission raise serious First Amendment issues, and court action in those cases is worth examining.

In addition, contemporary regulatory policy has, to a sub-stantial degree, been shaped by a half-century of court decisions. On some occasions, the courts have forced the Commission to greatly expand citizen participation in regulatory policymaking by interpreting rules of standing to include a broader "public interest." The courts, particularly the USCADC, have been extremely active in considering and deciding broadcasting cases, and the Commission cannot assume that its rulings will be un-challenged by public interest groups or by the courts. A number of the cases provided judges with an opportunity to make major statements about the appropriateness and scope of judicial review and the First Amendment's application to broadcasting. The judges' statements, often written in majority opinions, have the force of law and compel the Commission to carefully consider the courts' attitudes when making future decisions.

Of the seventeen court cases, approximately half reversed FCC decisions:

Seventeen cases
  USCADC   8 upheld FCC

                  8 reversed FCC

                  1 came from 3-judge district court and
                  went directly to Supreme Court

Supreme Court   2 upheld USCADC

6 reversed USCADC

7 denied certiorari

1 upheld 3-judge district court

1 upheld state supreme court

It would have been methodologically convenient if the court decisions yielded a clear pattern of judicial decision making. Perhaps the cases indicate little more than regularized judicial intervention; that in itself is significant. Because so many factors influence the outcome of a case, it is risky to assume certain reasons for a case being decided a particular way. After the cases are discussed, some tentative conclusions indicate that courts play a major role in determining how the broadcasting industry is regulated.

THE 1930s

Prior to the landmark case of the *National Broadcasting Company v. United States*[6] in 1943, the U.S. Court of Appeals and the Supreme Court considered a number of important cases dealing with programming and the extent to which the Commission could control the content of programs.

As stated before, the Federal Radio Act of 1927 and the Communications Act of 1934 demonstrated Congress' recognition that print and electronic media were not constitutionally parallel and that a certain amount of government control over radio was not only tolerable but also necessary. A few years after passage of the Federal Radio Act, the federal courts considered how the difference in the nature of the media would guide the Federal Radio Commission in exercising its licensing powers. In effect, the courts were faced with the difficult task of distinguishing the broadcasters' First Amendment rights from those of print journalists.

Two cases—one decided by the Supreme Court, the other decided by the U.S. Court of Appeals for the District of

Columbia—clearly illustrate early judicial intervention in regulatory policymaking. Considered together, the two cases demonstrate that the First Amendment did apply differently
to broadcasting.

Near v. Minnesota,[7] decided by a closely divided Supreme
Court in 1931, involved a "scandal sheet" published by
J. M. Near and a partner. They ran afoul of chapter 285 of the
Session Laws of Minnesota for the year 1925 providing for the
abatement, as a public nuisance, of a "malicious, scandalous and
defamatory newspaper, magazine or other periodical."[8]

Section 2 of the Act provided that whenever any such nuisance
is committed or exists any county attorney in whose district such
periodical is published or circulated "may maintain an action in
the district court of the county in the name of the State to
enjoin perpetually the persons committing or maintaining any
such nuisance from further committing or maintaining it."[9]
If a publisher disobeyed an injunction, he could be punished for
contempt of court.

Under this statute, the county attorney of Hennepin County
brought an action to enjoin the publication of what was
described as a "malicious, scandalous and defamatory newspaper, magazine and periodical," known as *The Saturday Press,*
published by the defendants in Minneapolis.

Because of the analogies to the broadcasting case mentioned
below, it is worth noting what Near printed that was so offensive
to state authorities:

The articles charged that a Jewish gangster was in control of gambling,
bootlegging and racketeering in Minneapolis, and that law enforcement
officials and agencies were not energetically performing their duties.[10]

Chief Justice Charles Evans Hughes, writing for a Court
divided 5-4, considered the significant question to be whether a
law authorizing such government action to restrain publication
squared with freedom of the press as historically conceived and
guaranteed.[11] To Hughes, it was a clear case of prior restraint. In
his opinion, he traced the history of the guarantee of freedom of
the press and concluded that previous restraint was unconstitutional, save for "exceptional cases such as publication of troop

movements in war time and incitements to acts of violence endangering the community." Hughes continued:

The fact that liberty of the press may be abused by miscreant purveyors of scandal does not make any the less necessary the immunity of the press from previous restraint in dealing with official misconduct. Subsequent punishment for such abuses as may exist is the appropriate remedy, consistent with constitutional privilege.[12]

To Justice Pierce Butler, dissenting with Justices Willis Van Devanter, James McReynolds, and George Sutherland, the Minnesota statute did not operate as a *previous*[13] restraint on publications:

There is nothing in the statute purporting to prohibit publications that have not been adjudged to constitute a nuisance. It is fanciful to suggest similarity between the granting or enforcement of the decree authorized by this statute to prevent *further*[14] publication of malicious, scandalous and defamatory articles and the previous restraint upon the press by the licensers as referred to by Blackstone and described in the history of the times to which he alludes.[15]

Despite these objections, Chief Justice Hughes made it clear that the First Amendment was intended to protect print journalists from prior restraint, which would be tolerated under only the rarest of circumstances.

Such was not the case with broadcasting. For a station licensed by the federal government, the ultimate act of prior restraint is to take away the broadcasting license, thereby forever silencing the voices that had used the frequency. In *Trinity Methodist Church South v. Federal Radio Commission*,[16] a year after *Near*, the U.S. Court of Appeals for the District of Columbia held that a radio license could be taken away for attacks very similar to those in *Near*.

The Reverend Doctor Schuler, licensee and operator of radio station KGEF in Los Angeles, filed to renew his license in 1930. Numerous citizens protested to the Federal Radio Commission.[17] The FRC denied Schuler's renewal on the grounds that his broadcasts attacked the Roman Catholic Church, were "sensational rather than instructive, and obstructed the orderly administration of public justice [he had been convicted of contempt for attacking judges]."[18] Schuler's church, Trinity Methodist, South, appealed the Commission's decision on the grounds that it violated free speech and due process.

Judge D. Lawrence Groner wrote the unanimous opinion for the five-judge panel of the U.S. Court of Appeals for the District of Columbia. The court held that Congress has the right to establish agencies to regulate the airwaves and that such agencies can refuse to renew licenses to those who have abused the license by broadcasting defamatory and untrue matter. Groner then discussed the kind of attacks that KGEF had broadcast and his view as to their effect:

If it be considered that one in possession of a permit to broadcast in interstate commerce may, without let or hindrance from any source, use these facilities, reaching out as they do, from one corner of the country to the other, to obstruct the administration of justice, offend the religious susceptibilities of thousands, inspire political distrust and civic discord, or offend youth and innocence by the use of words suggestive of sexual immorality, and be answerable for slander only at the instance of the one offended, then this great science, instead of boon, will become a scourge, and the nation a theatre for the display of individual passions and collision of personal interests. This is neither censorship nor previous restraint, nor is it a whittling away of the rights guaranteed by the First Amendment, or an impairment of their free exercise.[19]

The Supreme Court denied certiorari without comment.[20]

Considered together, *Near* and *Trinity* made it clear that a newspaper owner could not be stopped from publishing because he attacked public officials and religious groups but that a radio broadcaster could be silenced for making similiar attacks. The court in *Trinity* concluded that denying a license is merely the application of the regulatory power of Congress, not a violation of freedom of speech.

In another pre-Communications Act case, the U.S. Court of Appeals again sustained the Federal Radio Commission in a licensing case, *KFBK v. Federal Radio Commission.*[21] Judge Charles H. Robb, writing for a unanimous three-judge panel, held that the Commission was correct in denying renewal of a license of a Milford, Kansas, radio station owned by a Dr. J. R. Brinkley. The Commission had refused to renew the license because he used the station for personal use, devoting programming to diagnosing and treating medical cases from letters sent to the station.

The above cases dealing with the issues of program content, in which Commission action was affirmed by the courts, arose prior to passage of the Communications Act and were known to Congress when the Act was passed. Nevertheless, Congress chose to transfer the "public interest, convenience, or necessity" standard from the Federal Radio Act to the Communications Act, despite the vagueness of that standard and the corresponding discretion that had to be granted to the agency charged with deciding when it is served.

The courts in the 1930s, however, were not afraid to review Commission decisions; the U.S. Court of Appeals reversed the Commission in *Federal Radio Commission v. Nelson Brothers*,[22] decided in 1933. This case involved a station that had been denied renewal of its license and the frequency awarded to another applicant. The Court of Appeals for the District of Columbia, by a 3-2 vote, reversed the FRC decision, finding it, in the words of Judge Robb, "arbitrary and capricious."[23]

The Supreme Court, in reversing the Court of Appeals, reaffirmed the decision of the Commission. Chief Justice Hughes, writing for a unanimous Court, held that this was not a revocation of a license and that "the only question was distribution of frequencies."[24] The Court further held that, in pursuit of the "public interest, convenience, or necessity," it was not arbitrary to allocate frequencies at the expense of an existing station. It is significant that Hughes did not mention the issues raised by regulating program content or the First Amendment.

The 1930s saw a court system attempting to come to grips with a highly complex yet vital industry, the regulation of which invariably involved some constitutional issues. For the most part, the courts allowed the newly created FRC and FCC to find their way. But the courts did intervene when they felt that the Commissions had abused their statutory authority.

THE 1940s

The 1940s saw a number of extremely important court decisions that provided the judges with opportunities to discuss in detail broadcasting's relationship to government.

One of the most important cases considered by the Supreme Court was *Federal Communications Commission v. Pottsville Broadcasting Company*,[25] decided in 1940. Once again, the Supreme Court refused to tolerate the Court of Appeals' interference with an FCC decision.

While the issues in the case may have been confusing, Justice Felix Frankfurter's opinion for the Court was an essay on the relationship between courts and administrative agencies and an admonition to the judicial system to use extreme caution in adapting its procedures to administrative decisions. In praising the flexibility and expertise of administrative law, Justice Frankfurter warned against assuming that common law would apply to the important new area of administrative law.

In the *Pottsville* case, the petitioner had been denied a license because the Commission found him unqualified financially. On appeal, the Court of Appeals reversed and remanded, holding that the Commission, in appraising his financial qualifications, had made an error in interpreting state law.[26]

On remand, the Commission called for a comparative hearing in which other applicants for the frequency were considered along with the Pottsville Broadcasting Company. Pottsville then sought and was granted: (1) a writ of mandamus requiring the Commission to set aside its order denying its application and assigning it for rehearing with other applicants for the same frequency and (2) an order to the Commission to hear and reconsider the respondent's application on the basis of the record as originally made up when its application was first decided adversely by the Commission and brought before the court on appeal. For a unanimous three-judge panel, Judge Groner ordered the writ of mandamus but stayed it for thirty days to allow appeal to the Supreme Court.

A unanimous Supreme Court considered the Court of Appeals' action inappropriate and reversed the judgment ordering the writ of mandamus dissolved.

Justice Frankfurter opened his opinion with a brief history of broadcast regulation and discussed the principles of regulation as stated in the Federal Radio Act of 1927 and the Communications Act of 1934. He acknowledged that the standard "public interest, convenience or necessity" is as concrete as the complicated factors for judgment in such a field of delegated authority permit"[27] but that the standard "serves as a supple instrument for the exercise of discretion by the expert body which Congress has charged to carry out its legislative policy."[28]

Then, in a much-quoted passage, Justice Frankfurter reminded broadcasters that they acquire no ownership rights to the frequency:

It is highly significant that although investment in broadcasting stations may be large, a license may not be issued for more than three years; and in deciding whether to renew the license, just as in deciding whether to issue it in the first place, the Commission must judge by the standard of "public convenience, interest or necessity." The Communications Act is not designed primarily as a new code for the adjustment of conflicting private rights through adjudication. Rather it expresses a desire on the part of Congress to maintain, through appropriate administrative control, a grip on the dynamic aspects of radio transmission.[29]

In addition, Justice Frankfurter claimed that the public interest standard is not absolute, but comparative. The Commission, he believed, should enjoy wide discretion in interpreting that standard. If the Commission wanted to hold comparative hearings, the Supreme Court would allow it to do so and would not permit the Court of Appeals to interfere.

Justice Frankfurter also warned the Court of Appeals not to assume that its relationship with the Federal Communications Commission was identical to that of appellate federal courts to lower federal courts. The Court of Appeals invoked against the Commission the doctrine that a lower court is bound to respect the mandate of an appellate tribunal and cannot reconsider questions that the mandate has laid to rest. But, wrote Justice Frankfurter, the Federal Communications Commission is not a lower court that the U.S. Court of Appeals can instruct at will. Nor is the court's interpretation of the scope of its own mandate necessarily conclusive:

To be sure the court that issues a mandate is normally the best judge of its content, on the general theory that the author of a document is ordinarily the authoritative interpreter of its purposes. But it is not even true that a lower court's interpretation of its mandate is controlling here.[30]

To Justice Frankfurter, this was not a mandate from a court to a court, but a mandate from a court to an administrative agency. What is at issue, as he pointed out, is not the relationship of federal courts–"a relationship largely defined by the courts themselves–but the due observance by courts of the distribution of authority made by Congress as between its power to regulate commerce and the reviewing power which it has conferred upon the courts under Article III of the Constitution."[31] When rules of hierarchy are ap[p]lied to the administrative process those rules are applied out of context, according to Frankfurter. The judicial role must be limited when administrative agencies are exercising legitimate powers conferred by Congress.

Justice Frankfurter placed in the record a full statement of his attitude toward the role of administrative agencies. The relationship among courts and that among courts and administrative agencies are not analogous, and to make such an assertion is to "misunderstand the origin and purposes of the movement for administrative regulation and at the same time to disregard the traditional scope, however far reaching, of the judicial process."[32] He continued:

Unless these vital differentiations between the functions of judicial and administrative tribunals are observed, courts will stray outside their province and read the laws of Congress through the distorting lenses of inapplicable legal doctrine.[33]

The same year as *Pottsville*, the Supreme Court again argued for restraint in dealing with decisions and actions of administrative agencies by reversing the Court of Appeals and reaffirming the FCC. In *Federal Communications Commission v. Sanders Brothers Radio Station*,[34] the petitioner had protested the licensing of an additional station in his community on the ground that it would cause him economic injury. He had lost before the Commission, but the Court of Appeals had reversed because of the failure of the Commission to find on the economic injury issue.

The Supreme Court upheld the Commission in an opinion that once again sketched the general framework of broadcast regulation, emphasizing that the field is one of "free competition."[35] Justice Owen Roberts, for a unanimous Supreme Court,[36] concluded that the economic injury issue, although relevant to the public interest, convenience, and necessity, was not "in and of itself" a factor the Commission must weigh. Thus, the Court added economic injury to the equities that the Commission can override in pursuit of the public interest.[37]

In what was perhaps an offhand remark in the text of the opinion, not in a footnote, Justice Roberts set into law words that may have helped establish principles that were later to cause much controversy:

> But the [Communications] Act does not essay to regulate the business of the licensee. The Commission is given no supervisory control of the programs, of business management or of policy. In short, the broadcasting field is open to anyone, provided there be an available frequency over which he can broadcast without interference to others, if he shows his competency, the adequacy of his equipment, and financial ability to make good use of the assigned channel.[38]

One should not make too much of what might have been a casual remark. Justice Roberts did not command the respect afforded Justice Frankfurter, and many consider Justice Roberts' comments erased by Justice Frankfurter three years later in *National Broadcasting Company v. United States.* The remark, however, should not be ignored completely. It was made by a justice writing for a unanimous Court that included Frankfurter. Regardless of how seriously the comment was taken, it did identify principles that broadcasters would later use to argue for minimal government regulation of their industry.

Three years after *Sanders Brothers*, the Supreme Court considered the complex *NBC* case, which enabled two respected jurists to make major statements on communications law and government regulation: Justice Frankfurter writing for the majority, and Justice Frank Murphy providing an eloquent dissent. The issues raised in those opinions, moreover, make the case worthy of careful examination.

The case involved chain broadcasting regulations promulgated after elaborate and extensive hearings by the FCC and announced on May 2, 1941 and amended on October 11, 1941. NBC tried to enjoin enforcement of the regulations but was unsuccessful in the Court of Appeals, whose decision was affirmed by the Supreme Court.

The case involved a number of regulations dealing with such matters as control of local station rates by the network, network programs, network option-time provisions, the length of contract terms, and provisions for territorial exclusivity and exclusive affiliation. The issues reflected a blend of antitrust concerns and the question whether a station owner can delegate some of his responsibilities to the network.[39]

The Federal Communications Commission did not develop the rules casually. A committee of three commissioners held public hearings for seventy-three days over a six-month period. The order announcing the investigation and specifying the particular matters that would be explored at the hearings was published in the *Federal Register*, and copies were sent to every station licensee and network. Station licensees, national and regional networks, and other interested parties were invited to appear and give evidence. Ninety-six witnesses were heard by the committee, forty-five of whom were called by the national networks. The evidence covered 27 volumes, including over 8,000 pages of testimony and more than 700 exhibits.

Finally, after a number of interim actions, the Commission, on May 2, 1941, issued its report on chain broadcasting. On October 11, 1941, the Commission, with two commissioners dissenting, issued a supplemental report.

In Justice Frankfurter's detailed thirty-five page opinion, he reviewed the history of network development that led to the promulgation of the chain broadcasting rules. He listed the number of stations affiliated with each network at various times.[40]

The Commission had become concerned over the concentration of programming control in the hands of relatively few people and over the abdication of programming responsibility by the local licensee to the network. Justice Frankfurter, in referring to the Commission's report, recognized the importance of chain broadcasting, particularly because it makes possible wider reception for expensive entertainment and cultural programs and also for programs of national or regional significance that would be too expensive for local stations to produce. Furthermore, access to greatly enlarged audiences made possible by chain broadcasting has been a strong incentive to advertisers to finance the production of such programs. The Commission report continued:

But the fact that the chain broadcasting method brings benefits and advantages to both the listening public and to broadcast station licensees does not mean that the prevailing practices and policies of the networks and their outlets are sound in all respects, or that they should not be altered. The Commission's duty under the Communications Act of 1934 is not only to see that the public receives the advantages and benefits of chain broadcasting, but also, so far as its powers enable it, to see that practices which adversely affect the ability of licensees to operate in the public interest are eliminated.[41]

Within the powers granted to it by Congress, the Commission found a number of network abuses that were amenable to correction. They included problems raised by exclusive affiliation of stations, terms of affiliation, the right to reject network programs, network ownership of stations, and other issues that remain controversial today.

The *NBC* case is important because it found that the Commission, after lengthy hearings that included parties representing many different interests, was entitled to establish these rules without interference by the Court of Appeals or by the Supreme Court.

Justice Frankfurter, after a detailed review of the regulations themselves and of the legal history of broadcasting, turned to the key isssue: Had Congress authorized such rule making? There was much support for the argument that the Commission was limited to supervising the technical and financial aspects of broadcasting,[42] but Justice Frankfurter rejected such an argument. To him, the Commission was more than just a "traffic cop":

The Act itself establishes that the Commission's powers are not limited to the engineering and technical aspects of regulation of radio communication. Yet we are asked to regard the Commission as kind of a traffic officer, policing the wave lengths to prevent stations from interfering with each other. But the Act does not restrict the Commission merely to supervision of traffic. It puts upon the Commission the burden of determining the composition of that traffic. The facilities of radio are not large enough to accommodate all who wish to use them. Methods must be devised for choosing among the many who apply. And since Congress itself could not do this, it committed the task to the Commission.[43]

The Court's opinion in *NBC* does not clearly indicate whether it was merely interpreting statutory law or was, in fact, further clarifying what constitutional mandate binds the Commission in its duty to regulate broadcasting. In *NBC*, the Court was called on to consider whether the chain broadcasting rules, as promulgated by the Commission, were within the statutory authority provided by the Communications Act. Considering the elaborate hearings that were held prior to the Commission's final decision, the Court of Appeals or the Supreme Court would have found it extremely difficult to have upset those rules on *due process* grounds. That does not mean, of course, that the Commission need only hear a certain number of witnesses and compile a certain number of pages of testimony for the courts to meekly approve its decisions. On the other hand, *NBC* clearly demonstrated that the Supreme Court does not consider the Court of Appeals or itself to be a "Super-FCC," disturbing decisions of that agency whenever the fancy strikes it.

The Court, in rejecting the argument that the FCC is no more than a traffic cop, did not suggest what criteria beyond financial and engineering that the Commission may consider. To do so would have been contradictory to Justice Frankfurter's belief that courts should play a limited role in administrative affairs and should intervene only when the constitutional issues are so compelling that the Court cannot remain silent.

The First Amendment received scant attention in Justice Frankfurter's opinion. The petitioners, after attacking the regulations on other grounds, threw in an appeal on First Amendment grounds as a last resort. It is noteworthy that Justice Frankfurter did not consider the First Amendment issues until the next to last paragraph of his opinion, and he dismissed them quickly:

> We come, finally, to an appeal to the First Amendment. The regulations, even if valid in all other respects, must fall because they abridge, say the appellants, their right of free speech. If that be so, it would follow that every person whose application for a license to operate a station is denied by the Commission is thereby denied his constitutional right of free speech. Freedom of utterance is abridged to many who wish to use the limited facilities of radio. Unlike other modes of expression, radio inherently is not available to all. That is its unique characteristic, and that is why, unlike other modes of expression, it is subject to governmental regulation. Because it cannot be used by all, some who wish to use it must be denied.[44]

Justice Frankfurter's words raised more questions than they answered. The petitioners were surely not arguing that radio could not be licensed at all because of the First Amendment; yet that is the position to which Justice Frankfurter appeared to respond.[45] Nor can he be suggesting that because the facilities of radio are limited broadcasting, unlike other modes of communication, is subject to unlimited governmental regulation. Yet that was what he came close to saying.

Later in the same paragraph, Justice Frankfurter attempted to calm those worried about such government regulation:

> But Congress did not authorize the Commission to choose among applicants upon the basis of their political, economic, or social views, or upon any other capricious basis. If it did, or if the Commission by these regulations proposed a choice among applicants upon some such basis, the issue before us would be wholly different.[46]

Since these conditions were not present, he postponed a decision regarding Commission regulation of certain aspects of broadcasting. For now, the issue was the regulations, not freedom of speech. He was careful to warn the Commission not to judge otherwise equally qualified applicants on the basis of their political views. But he provided little insight into the role that freedom of speech guarantees, as historically conceived, should play in moderating and guiding FCC decision making.

If Justice Frankfurter gave the First Amendment little attention in his opinion, Justice Murphy, despite his reputation as being second to none in sensitivity to free speech issues, chose not to refer directly to it at all in his dissent. Such an omission could not have been accidental. His main concern was that the Court majority had bestowed upon an administrative agency power that Congress had not granted it. "Since that is what the Court in substance does today, I dissent."[47]

Justice Murphy considered the issue in *NBC* to be extremely important. He expressed concern over what happens to a nation when its press is controlled by government, illustrating his point by citing use of radio in Europe as a weapon of "authority and misrepresentation," not as a vehicle of entertainment and enlightenment.

Because of the nature of broadcasting, Congress was forced to vest a considerable amount of discretionary authority in the Commission, Justice Murphy acknowledged. But, he claimed, the Commission had exercised power it did not rightly possess. In the *NBC* case, the Commission's real objective was to

regulate the business practices of the major networks, thus bringing within the range of its regulatory power the chain broadcasting industry as a whole. By means of these regulations and the enforcement program, the Commission would not only extend its authority over business activities which represent interests and investments of a very substantial character, which have not been put under its jurisdiction by the Act, but would greatly enlarge its control over an institution that has now become a rival of the press and pulpit as a purveyor of news and entertainment and a medium of public discussion.

To assume a function and responsibility of such wide reach and importance in the life of the nation, as a mere incident of its duty to pass on individual applications for permission to operate a radio station and use a specific wave length, is an assumption of authority to which I am not willing to lend my assent.[48]

Justice Roberts concurred with Justice Murphy that the Supreme Court had allowed the Commission to assume power that it had not been granted by Congress. The dissenters claimed that specific sections of the Communications Act clearly stated congressional intentions on safeguarding radio broadcasting arrangements that are deemed objectionable because of monopolistic or other features, and no remedy is available under the Act by which the Commission could curtail such practices. According to the dissenters, any remedy should come from Congress in the form of legislation, not from the Commission exercising implied powers.

Both procedurally and substantively, *NBC v. United States* was the most important case to arise amid the controversy surrounding the Commission's chain broadcasting regulations. Two other cases, however, raised procedural questions that helped clarify the Supreme Court's position on the proper role of the courts in administrative matters.

One of the oldest canons of judicial review[49] is that an appellate court will refrain from interfering with a decision or controversy until the agency below, whether a lower court or administrative tribunal, has made a "final" decision. It is highly significant, therefore, that in *Columbia Broadcasting System v. United States*,[50] a 1942 case that later became part of the *NBC* case, the Supreme Court acted before that "final" decision.

Chief Justice Harlan Stone, over the objections of Justices Frankfurter, William Douglas, and Stanley Reed,[51] held that radio stations were compelled to follow the regulations as soon as they were issued and that the U.S. Court of Appeals did not have to wait for administrative action before making a determination as to the rights of persons affected by the regulations:

The ultimate test of reviewability is not to be found in an overrefined technique, but in the need of the review to protect from the irreparable injury threatened in the exceptional case by administrative rulings which attach legal consequences to action taken in advance of other hearings and adjudications that may follow, the results of which the regulations purport to control.[52]

Justice Frankfurter, speaking also for Justices Douglas and Reed, criticized the Court majority for advocating court intervention that he considered unwarranted:

To say that the courts should reject the doctrine of administrative finality and take jurisdiction whenever action of an administrative agency may seriously affect substantial business interests, regardless of how intermediate or incomplete the action may be, is in effect, to imply that the protection of legal interests is entrusted solely to the courts.[53]

Justice Frankfurter's position in the *CBS* case appeared to be inconsistent with his majority opinion in *Scripps-Howard Radio v. Federal Communications Commission*,[54] decided only two months earlier. Despite the fact that he had argued that courts should play a limited role in reviewing FCC decisions, he wrote for a Court majority that the Communications Act entitled the Court of Appeals for the District of Columbia to stay orders of the Commission from which an appeal is taken, pending the determination of that appeal. Justice Douglas, in dissent, claimed that section 402 (b) of the Communications Act granted the Court of Appeals power to stay certain Commission orders but not those in the *Scripps* case. He criticized the Court majority for extending the scope of judicial review beyond what Congress had intended: "When Congress in one section of an Act has provided for a stay of certain orders but not of others, it has not remained silent on the subject."[55]

While the Court in *CBS* and *Scripps* appeared to define an active role for courts in reviewing FCC decisions, Justice Frankfurter and the Court in the *NBC* case suggested a more limited judicial role.

Three years after *NBC*, the Supreme Court again refused to condone Court of Appeals interference with a controversial FCC decision denying license renewal to a station that had misrepresented its financial arrangements.

Justice Robert Jackson, writing for a unanimous Court in

Federal Communications Commission v. WOKO,[56] agreed with a dissenting judge from the Court of Appeals "that this is a hard case" but nevertheless instructed the Court of Appeals to defer to the judgment of the FCC.

Over a period of twelve years, the company that owned WOKO concealed the fact that a vice-president of CBS, Sam Pickard, and his family, owned 240 shares, or 24 percent, of the company's outstanding stock. Apparently, the names were concealed because Pickard had obtained the stock to assist WOKO in securing affiliation with CBS, to furnish, without charge, engineers from CBS to construct the station at Albany, New York, and to supply a grand piano and certain newspaper publicity.[57] Obviously, Pickard did not want his colleagues at CBS to know about his financial holdings at WOKO.

By a 2-1 vote, the U.S. Court of Appeals reversed the Commission's decision to deny renewal of WOKO's license. [58] The majority held that the Commission had acted contrary to its decisions in similar cases, that the Commission had failed to find that the concealment was material, or that the Commission would have acted differently had it known the true owners of the stock.

Justice Jackson dismissed those arguments and chided the Court of Appeals for reviewing issues that he believed did not fall within appropriate statutes defining the scope of review. He felt that the Commission was correct in considering the issue of concealment:

> The fact of concealment may be more significant than the facts concealed. The willingness to deceive a regulatory body may be disclosed by immaterial and useless deceptions as well as by material and persuasive ones. We do not think it is an answer to say that the deception was unnecessary and served no purpose.[59]

Justice Jackson and the Court were unpersuaded that, because the majority stockholders were not found to have had any part in or knowledge of the concealment or deception, the company should have its license renewed if new executive officers managed the company. The Commission, according to the Court, was entitled to wide discretion in weighing such factors:

> This may be a very proper consideration for the Commission in determining just and appropriate action. But as matter of law, the fact that there are innocent stockholders cannot immunize the corporation from the consequences of such deception. If officers of the corporation by such mismanagement waste its assets, presumably the State law affords adequate remedies against the wrongdoers. . . . Consequences of such acts cannot be escaped by a corporation merely because not all of its stockholders participated.[60]

Although regulatory agencies are not bound by such formal rules as *stare decisis*, which theoretically govern courts, they are essentially adjudicative bodies and are required to be relatively uniform in their decisions affecting cases with similar circumstances. But Justice Jackson warned that agencies were to be allowed wide discretion and that the courts could not decide when the Commission was being consistent:

> Respondent complains that the present case constitutes a departure from the course which the Commission has taken in dealing with misstatements and applications in other cases. Much is made in argument of the fact that deceptions of this character have not been uncommon and it claimed that they have not been dealt with so severely as in this case. . . . The mild measures to others and the apparently unannounced change of policy are considerations appropriate for the Commission in determining whether its action in this case was too drastic, but we cannot say that the Commission is bound by anything that appears before us to deal with all cases at all times as it has dealt with some that seem comparable.[61]

Finally, Justice Jackson, addressing the issue of court involvement in reviewing FCC decisions, appeared to scold the Court of Appeals for second guessing the Commission in what some might describe as a "judgment call":

> It may very well be that this Station has established such a standard of public service that the Commission would be justified in considering that its deception was not a matter that affected its qualifications to serve the public. But it is the Commission, not the courts, which must

be satisfied that the public interest will be served by renewing the license. And the fact that we might not have made the same determination on the same facts does not warrant a substitution of judicial for administrative discretion since Congress has confided the problem to the latter. We agree that this is a hard case, but we cannot agree that it should be allowed to make bad law.[62]

Despite Justice Jackson's warning to courts not to substitute their judgment for that of the Commission, the courts, particularly the U.S. Court of Appeals for the District of Columbia, have not assumed such a limited role and have reversed Commission decisions in areas that historically have been within the jurisdiction of the Commission. The court has even ordered the Commission to take away a license it had renewed, in the process lambasting the Commission for its handling of the case and its favoritism toward existing licensees with some of the strongest language ever leveled at an administrative agency.[63]

In summary, in the 1940s the courts attempted to deal with a number of complex broadcasting cases. If there was a theme, it was one of paradox: while a number of Supreme Court justices argued for restraint on the part of courts and deference to the Commission, the U.S. Court of Appeals nonetheless reversed the Commission in three out of the four cases presented above. In two other cases, however, the Supreme Court approved a much greater level of court involvement in FCC decisions. As was seen in *Columbia Broadcasting v. United States*,[64] no less respected a jurist than Chief Justice Stone held for the majority that the Court of Appeals did not have to wait for a "final" decision in a case before making its determination. And in *Scripps-Howard Radio v. Federal Communications Commission*,[65] a majority held that Congress gave the Court of Appeals the power to stay certain Commission orders until a determination is made on appeal. Significantly, however, in each of the three cases where the Court of Appeals reversed the decisions of the Commission, the Supreme Court restored them. While such a conclusion must be tentative, during the 1940s, the courts allowed the Commission to "find its way" but also had assumed a more active role that included disturbing Commission decisions in complex and important cases.

THE 1950s

It fell to Justice Frankfurter to repeat his statements from the 1940s about the proper role of courts in reviewing Commission decisions. In a 1953 case, *Federal Communications Commission v. RCA Communications*,[66] he seemed to say that courts should limit their scope of review to the *process* by which decisions are made and should exercise restraint when reviewing the content of those decisions:

> Ours is not the duty of reviewing determinations of "fact," in the narrow, colloquial scope of that concept. Congress has charged the courts with the responsibility of saying whether the Commission has fairly exercised its discretion within the vaguish, penumbral bounds expressed by the standard of "public interest." It is our responsibility to say whether the Commission has been guided by proper considerations in bringing the deposit of its experience, the disciplined feel of the expert, to bear on applications for licenses in the public interest.[67]

The *RCA* case was a clear restatement, over a dozen years after *Pottsville*, that the courts should exercise restraint in reviewing the rulings of regulatory agencies.

But a year later, in *Federal Communications Commission v. American Broadcasting Company*,[68] decided in 1954, the Supreme Court itself was to ignore Justice Frankfurter's advice and reject a claim of Commission authority.

At issue were FCC rules prohibiting "give-away" programs. Chief Justice Earl Warren, for a unanimous Court,[69] invalidated the rules, holding that the programs at issue were not "lotteries" within the statutory prohibition and that the Commission, therefore, exceeded its rule-making powers as defined in the Communications Act.[70]

The case dealt only indirectly with program content; the issue was simply what constituted a lottery. But it did indicate that there were limits to Commission power.[71]

The only other case from the 1950s considered here did not involve an FCC or a Court of Appeals ruling, but it did provide one of the great First Amendment scholars, Justice Hugo Black, an opportunity to comment on the constitutionality of one of the most important provisions of the Communications Act, section 315.

The Court, divided 5-4, with Justice Frankfurter dissenting, held that the equal time mandate of section 315 coupled with the prohibition against editing section 315 broadcasts[72] suspend state law making a station liable for defamation. Justice Black, writing for the majority, reasoned that because of federal policy the station owner had been left helpless to protect himself. In discussing section 315, Justice Black appeared to concede its constitutionality:

> While denying all candidates the use of stations would protect broadcasters from liability, it would also effectively withdraw political discussion from the air. Instead the thrust of Section 315 is to facilitate political debate over radio and television. . . . Certainly Congress knew the obvious that if a licensee could protect himself in no other way but by refusing to broadcast candidates' speeches, the necessary effect would be to hamper the congressional plan to develop broadcasting as a political outlet, rather than to foster it.[73]

Justice Frankfurter dissented, writing that the Court had invalidated a state law by "hypothesizing congressional acquiescence and by supposing 'conflicting' state law which we cannot be certain exists and which, if it does exist, is not incompatible with federal law."[74] Justice Frankfurter would have reversed the North Dakota Supreme Court and remanded the case to it with instructions that "Section 315 has left the States the power to determine the nature and extent of liability, if any, of broadcasters to third persons."[75] It is interesting that Justice Black, with his reputation for strict interpretation of the First Amendment, did seem to approve of the purposes of section 315, if not its constitutionality.

The cases discussed in this chapter have traced the development of court involvement in shaping regulatory policy. If the courts were reluctant in the 1930s to be actively involved in broadcasting cases, they had by the 1950s become active participants in regulatory policymaking. During the period covered in this chapter, the Federal Communications Commission realized that it would have to contend with the courts when making important decisions. In the decades that followed, the courts assumed a role of unprecedented involvement that sets the stage for contemporary court-FCC relations.

NOTES

1. The safeguards will be discussed in chapter 4.

2. See *Schenck v. U.S.* (1919), *Abrams v. U.S.* (1919), *Gitlow v. New York* (1925), *Whitney v. California* (1927), and *Near v. Minnesota* (1931) as examples.

3. In this chapter, that court will occasionally be referred to as "USCADC."

4. For examples outside the communications field where a more general public interest was denied access, see *Sierra Club v. Morton* (1972) and *Warth v. Seldin* (1975).

5. 60 Stat. 324. Reprinted in Frederick C. Mosher, *Basic Documents of American Public Administration, 1776-1950* (New York: Holmes & Meier Publishers, Inc., 1976), pp. 182-91.

6. 319 U.S. 190.

7. 283 U.S. 697.

8. Gerald Gunther, *Individual Rights in Constitutional Law: Cases and Materials* (Mineola, N.Y.: The Foundation Press, 1976), p. 919.

9. Gunther, p. 919.

10. 283 U.S. at 704.

11. Harold L. Nelson and Dwight L. Teeter, Jr., *Law of Mass Communications: Freedom and Control of Print and Broadcast Media* (Mineola, N.Y.: The Foundation Press, Inc., 1969), p. 409.

12. Gunther, p. 922.

13. His emphasis.

14. His emphasis.

15. Gunther, p. 923.

16. 62 F.2d 850 (1932).

17. Nelson and Teeter, p. 410.

18. Ibid.

19. 62 F.2d at 852-53.

20. 284 U.S. 685 (1932).

21. 47 F.2d 670 (1932)

22. 289 U.S. 266 (1933).

23. 62 F.2d at 854.

24. 289 U.S. 266.

25. 309 U.S. 134 (1940).

26. 105 F. 2d 36 (1939).

27. 309 U.S. at 138.

28. Ibid.

29. Ibid.

30. 309 U.S. at 141.

31. Ibid.

32. Ibid., p. 144.

33. Ibid.

34. Ibid., p. 470.

35. Harry Kalven, Jr., "Broadcasting, Public Policy and the First Amendment,"

10 *The Journal of Law and Economics* (October 1967); 39.

   36. McReynolds took no part in the case.

   37. Kalven, p. 39.

   38. 309 U.S. at 475.

   39. Kalven, p. 42.

   40. 319 U.S. at 197.

   41. Ibid., p. 198.

   42. Kalven, p. 42.

   43. 319 U.S. at 215.

   44. Ibid., p. 226.

   45. Kalven, p. 44.

   46. 319 U.S. at 226.

   47. Ibid., pp. 227-28.

   48. Ibid.

   49. C. Herman Pritchett, *The Roosevelt Court* (Chicago: Quadrangle Books, 1948), p. 180.

   50. 316 U.S. 407.

   51. Black did not participate.

   52. 316 U.S. at 425.

   53. Ibid., p. 446.

   54. 316 U.S. 4 (1942).

   55. Ibid., p. 22.

   56. 329 U.S. 223 (1946).

   57. Ibid., p. 225.

   58. 153 F.2d 623.

   59. 329 U.S. at 227.

   60. Ibid.

   61. Ibid., pp. 227-28.

   62. Ibid., p. 229.

   63. *Office of Communication of the United Church of Christ v. Federal Communications Commission,* 359 F.2d 994 (1966).

   64. 316 U.S. 407.

   65. 316 U.S. 4 (1942).

   66. 346 U.S. 86 (1953).

   67. Ibid., p. 91.

   68. 347 U.S. 284.

   69. Douglas did not participate.

   70. 347 U.S. 284.

   71. The Supreme Court sustained an injunction from a three-judge District Court in the Southern District of New York, 11 F. Supp. 374.

   72. *Farmers Educational & Cooperative Union of America v. WDAY,* 360 U.S. 525 (1959). A station cannot edit material submitted under section 315.

   73. Ibid., pp. 534-35.

   74. Ibid., pp. 546-47.

   75. Ibid.

3.

The Courts and Broadcast Regulation: 1960 to the Present

In the 1960s and 1970s, the federal courts considered some of the most important and complex cases ever to arise from the regulation of the broadcasting industry. The courts further defined the scope of broadcasters' First Amendment rights and made it clear that they stood ready to intervene in controversial and technical cases. By relaxing rules of "standing," they allowed participation in regulatory proceedings by viewers and listeners who otherwise would have been barred. More importantly, the activist role sparked discussion of whether the courts have inappropriately crossed the boundary between judicial review and outright supervision of the Commission.

THE 1960s—[1]

The 1960s witnessed a major upheaval in American society. Blacks, particularly in the South, asserted their civil rights despite the hostility of many of the broadcasters in that region.

A television station in Jackson, Mississippi, was operated by a notorious segregationist who used his station to fight advancement of black citizens. He broadcast spot announcements urging resistance to integration because "Communists were behind the effort; he swore that James Meredith would never be admitted to the University of Mississippi; and whenever a black was featured on a network program, WLBT would interrupt with a slide that said, 'Sorry, Cable Trouble.' ''[2]

The station's track record was clear: over a period of nearly a decade since 1955, the station had consistently broadcast anti-integration and antiblack programs and remarks and had refused to allow spokesmen to rebut those comments. There were apparently only two occasions on which blacks had been on television in Mississippi despite the fact that they constituted 45 percent of the population.

Two local leaders, both associated with the United Church of Christ, petitioned the FCC to deny WLBT's license because the station violated the fairness doctrine by failing to provide for appearances by blacks while presenting controversial issues of public importance. Before the case was over, the United Church of Christ was to spend $240,000 on litigation, and the U.S. Court of Appeals for the District of Columbia was to excoriate the FCC for its handling of the case.[3]

In order to establish standing, Dr. Aaron Henry, Robert Smith, and the church claimed that they represented individuals and organizations that, in violation of the fairness doctrine, were denied a reasonable opportunity to be heard and were ignored and discriminated against in the station's programming.

The FCC ruled that Henry, Smith, and the United Church of Christ had no legal standing to intervene. However, the Commission felt it ought to look into the matters brought to its attention. Without holding any hearings to resolve the issues, it granted WLBT a one-year license renewal. The reason given by the Commission was that the area served by the station was entering a critical period in race relations and that

the broadcast stations, such as here involved, can make a most worthwhile contribution to the resolution of problems arising in this respect. That contribution is needed now—and should not be put off for the future. We believe that the licensee, operating in strict accordance with the representations made and other conditions specified herein, can make that needed contribution, and thus that its renewal would be in the public interest.[4]

Only two commissioners dissented from the decision to renew WLBT's license for a year without holding hearings.

The United Church of Christ and Reverend Everett Parker, a minister of the church in New York City, asked the Court of Appeals to overturn the FCC's decision, and the case was argued on December 3, 1965, before Judges Warren E. Burger, Carl McGowan, and Edward Tamm.

What followed in the next six years was one of the most bitter fights over any licensing decision between the Federal Communications Commission and a federal court. The legal exchanges were to be highlighted by some of the sternest language a court has ever directed at a regulatory agency, and for the first time in history, a United States court had in effect ordered the termination of a license in any of the regulated fields—railroads, airlines, telephone service, public utilities, and others.[5]

Interestingly, in the unanimous opinion of the Court of Appeals, Judge Burger was to be highly critical of the Commission for not relaxing its rules of standing to allow Henry and Smith to intervene. Later as Chief Justice of the United States, Burger would embark on a campaign to close the federal courts to public interest litigants, and the Supreme Court, with his encouragement, has made strides in that direction.[6]

Nevertheless, the Warren Burger of the Court of Appeals was of a different opinion about the role of the public in actions before the Commission. At that time, Judge Burger saw no reason to exclude "those with such an obvious and acute concern as the listening audience. This much seems essential to insure that the holders of broadcasting licenses be responsive to the needs of the audience, without which the broadcaster could not exist."[7]

Judge Burger then detailed the history of standing of members of the public before administrative agencies:

Under our system, the interests of the public are dominant. The commercial needs of licensed broadcasters and advertisers must be integrated into those of the public. Hence, individual citizens and the communities they compose owe a duty to themselves and their peers to take an active interest in the scope and quality of the television service which stations and networks provide and which, undoubtedly, has a vast impact on their lives and the lives of their children. Nor need the public feel that in taking a hand in broadcasting they are unduly interfering in the private business affairs of others. On the contrary, their interest in television programming is direct and their responsibilities important. They are the owners of the channels of television—indeed of all broadcasting.[8]

The opinion of the court on the issue of standing had significance far beyond the *WLBT* case. It opened the door to a new era in which public groups have standing to petition the Federal Communications Commission.

To some observers, the court's attitude on standing in the *WLBT* case has led to increased court involvement in broadcasting cases in response to the "emergence of the public-interest voice in broadcasting affairs."[9] Whatever the impetus for court intervention, there can be little argument as to its existence.

In 1966, the Court of Appeals directed the Commission to conduct hearings on WLBT's renewal application and to allow public intervention. In addition, Judge Burger specifically noted:

> We hold that the grant of a renewal of WLBT's license for one year was erroneous. The Commission is directed to conduct hearings on WLBT's renewal application, allowing public intervention pursuant to this holding. Since the Commission has already decided that Appellants are responsible representatives of the listening public of the Jackson area, we see no obstacle to a prompt determination granting standing to Appellants or some of them.[10]

On remand, the Commission took more than two years to consider seriously whether WLBT should continue to have the license, and while the Commission was taking a long look, WLBT began to improve its record.[11]

On June 27, 1968, the Commission, obviously convinced of the "good faith" effort to improve coverage of the black community, renewed WLBT's license for a full term of three years.

As five of the seven commissioners put it:

> We caution, however, against any conclusion that WLBT's performance . . . was spotless, or a model of perfection to be emulated by other stations. . . . We only conclude that the intervenors have failed to prove their charges and that the preponderance of the evidence before us establishes that station WLBT has afforded reasonable opportunity for the use of its facilities by the significant community groups comprising its service area.[12]

Then in a key passage, the five commissioners further held:

That the intervenors [Smith and Henry and the United Church of Christ] had not met their burden of proof on several issues like "Sorry, Cable Trouble," and that recent "marked improvements" in WLBT's local programming had been a positive factor.[13]

A year later, Judge Burger, speaking for the Court of Appeals, said that the Commission had come close to contempt of court. He made it clear that he did not expect regulatory agencies to ignore directives from the Court of Appeals:

The practical effect of the Commission's action was to place on the Public Intervenors the entire burden of showing that the licensee was not qualified to be granted a renewal. The Examiner and the Commission exhibited at best a reluctant tolerance of this court's mandate and at worst a profound hostility to the participation of the Public Intervenors and their efforts.

The record now before us leaves us with a profound concern over the entire handling of this case following the remand to the Commission. The impatience with the Public Intervenors, the hostility toward their efforts to satisfy a surprisingly strict standard of proof, plain errors in rulings and findings lead us, albeit reluctantly, to the conclusion that it will serve no useful purpose to ask the Commission to reconsider the Examiner's actions and its own Decision and Order under a correct allocation of the burden of proof. The administrative conduct reflected in this record is beyond repair.[14]

The case was remanded to the Commission, and in June 1971, the owner, Lamar Life Broadcasting, lost its license to broadcast over station WLBT.

In his opinion, Judge Burger spoke of the value of public interest litigants in monitoring the activities of radio and television stations and in reporting their findings to the Commission, which, because of insufficient resources and staff, is unable to conduct such monitorings itself. Judge Burger likened a public intervenor, as in this case, to a "complaining witness who presents evidence to the police or a prosecutor whose duty it is to conduct an affirmative and objective investigation of all the facts and pursue his prosecutorial or regulatory function if there is probable cause to believe a violation has occurred."[15]

The court vacated the grant of the license and directed the Commission to invite applications to be filed for the frequency. The court did allow Lamar Life Broadcasting to be one of the competing applicants, softening somewhat its mandate to the Commission, because, upon issuing an order refusing to hear *en banc* an appeal, Judges McGowan and Tamm recognized that the

ineptitude of the Commission was as much, if not more, to blame for this scandalous delay than was the licensee. For this reason . . . [the court] was not disposed to declare the licensee ineligible to seek new authority to use the channel.[16]

The judges appeared to recognize a Commission concern that the court had assumed the power to overrule the FCC in a most crucial area, license renewal. Because of such concern, the court allowed the Commission to ''voluntarily'' decide that Lamar Life should lose its license and that it should be given to another applicant.

Of all the cases considered in chapters 2 and 3, nowhere does a federal court use stronger language in striking down an FCC decision and in instructing the Commission on how to comply with the court's decision. The tone of Judge Burger's opinion suggested that he did not consider whether the court had exceeded its jurisdiction in dealing with the Commission. One gets the impression that when the Commission so clearly fails to act in the public interest by favoring existing licensees the court defines its own jurisdiction, and unless the Supreme Court intervenes, the Commission is required to follow the court's instructions. In this case, the Supreme Court denied certiorari.

The *WLBT* case illustrates a serious problem with the FCC, whose commissioners and staff enjoy frequent contact and close relations with those whom they are supposed to regulate. For various reasons, they appear to be greatly influenced by established broadcasting interests even when those interests conflict with claims pressed by public interest groups or new applicants for a frequency. Nowhere is bias toward established broadcasting interests better illustrated than in the *WLBT* case.

Perhaps the Court of Appeals' message was not lost on the Commission because two years later, the Commission took away Brandywine-Main Line's radio license to operate radio station WXUR in Media, Pennsylvania.[17]

It was a few years after *WLBT* that the most "famous" broadcasting case reached the Supreme Court. *Red Lion Broadcasting Company v. Federal Communications Commission*,[18] despite its fame and controversy, dealt with relatively simple issues. It was, however, the first time that the Supreme Court ruled directly on the constitutionality of the fairness doctrine.

At 1:12 PM on November 25, 1964, radio station WGCB in Red Lion, Pennsylvania, played a tape of Reverend Billy James Hargis, an Oklahoma evangelist preacher. In the program, Hargis delivered a stinging personal attack against Fred J. Cook, an investigative reporter whom Hargis considered too liberal. Hargis was outraged by Cook's book, *Goldwater: Extremist on the Right*, and he called Cook a "professional mudslinger," accusing him of dishonesty, of falsifying stories, and of defending Alger Hiss.[19]

The Hargis attack lasted less than two minutes, but the constitutional debate it sparked continues today. Five years after the program aired on WGCB, the Supreme Court held that the personal attack sections of the fairness doctrine were constitutional and that Cook was entitled to free time in which to reply to the attack.

Shortly after Cook complained to the FCC, the Commission ordered the station's owner, Reverend John Norris, to comply with the personal attack rules and to provide reply time to Cook. The dispute could have ended at that point, with Norris agreeing to comply with the FCC order and asking Cook to send a taped reply to WGCB.

But that was not what happened. Norris refused to accept the FCC's finding that he was a public trustee and proxy of the public's interest rather than the owner of the franchise.[20] Norris vowed to fight and the legal battle began.

The broadcasters, represented by the National Association of Broadcasters (NAB), were concerned that *Red Lion* would make a poor test case to challenge the constitutionality of the fairness doctrine. So on July 27, 1967, NAB, combined with the Radio and Television News Directors Association (RTNDA), filed a separate action challenging the fairness doctrine in the Seventh Circuit Court of Appeals in Chicago, which they found to be a suitable environment. On the same day, CBS filed its challenge in the Second Circuit in New York. NBC filed a few days later.

The suits were consolidated, and because it was the court where the case was filed first, the Seventh Circuit was awarded jurisdiction. So actually, two cases were being considered by the Supreme Court: *Red Lion* and *RTNDA-NBC-CBS*.

The Supreme Court announced its decision on June 9, 1969. The decision of the U.S. Court of Appeals for the District of Columbia was affirmed (the *Red Lion* case), and the U.S. Court of Appeals for the Seventh Circuit was reversed and the case remanded (*RTNDA-NBC-CBS*). Because the cases were consolidated in the Supreme Court, it is not necessary to discuss the lower court opinions.

Justice Byron White, speaking for a unanimous Supreme Court, began his opinion with a history of the fairness doctrine, particularly the personal attack and equal time provisions. He concluded that the application of the fairness doctrine in *Red Lion* and the promulgation of the regulations in *RTNDA* are both authorized by Congress and "enhance rather than abridge" freedoms of speech and press protected by the First Amendment.

To Justice White, this was the proper exercise of Commission authority:

The history of the mergence of the fairness doctrine and of the related legislation shows that the Commission's action in the *Red Lion* case did not exceed its authority, and that in adopting the new regulations the Commission was implementing congressional policy rather than embarking on a frolic of its own.[21]

The Court held that the 1959 Amendments to the Communications Act included the fairness doctrine in the "public interest" standard[22] as established in the Federal Radio Act and carried forward to the Communications Act. This decision was extremely significant because in effect it gave the Commission wide discretion in ordering stations to make reply time available as part of their public interest responsibilities. The Court appeared to be saying that, if the Commission based directives for reply time on general public interest grounds, rather than on specific provisions of the fairness doctrine, the Commission would be granted broad discretion to interpret the public interest standard and how reply time would serve it.

The Court then turned to the First Amendment's relationship to broadcasting:

> When there are substantially more individuals who want to broadcast than there are frequencies to allocate, it is idle to posit an unabridgeable First Amendment right to broadcast comparable to the right of every individual to speak, write, or publish.[23]

Justice White acknowledged that the First Amendment is not irrelevant to broadcasting and that it has a major role to play, as Congress itself recognized in various sections of the Communications Act, but

> because of the scarcity of radio frequencies, the Government is permitted to put restraints on licensees in favor of others whose views should be expressed on this unique medium. But the people as a whole retain their interest in free speech by radio and their collective right to have the medium function consistently with the ends and purposes of the First Amendment. It is the right of the viewers and listeners, not the right of the broadcasters, which is paramount.[24]

This view of the First Amendment as it applies to broadcasting allows the First Amendment to preserve an uninhibited market-place of ideas in which truth will ultimately prevail, according to the Court, and it helps prevent monopolization by either the government or private individuals.

Justice White dismissed as unfounded the concern that approving the constitutionality of the personal attack provisions and the fairness doctrine generally will cause self-censorship among the media. He indicated that such fears are speculative and that the fairness doctrine in the past "has had no such effect."[25] The rules are carefully drawn, according to Justice White, and do not raise serious First Amendment issues:

> They assert that under specified circumstances, a licensee must offer to make available a reasonable amount of broadcast time to those who

have a view different from that which has already been expressed on his station. . . . The First Amendment confers no right on licensees to prevent others from broadcasting on "their" frequencies and no right to an unconditional monopoly of a scarce resource which the Government has denied others the right to use.[26]

Justice White warned that *Red Lion* should not be understood to mean that the Supreme Court approves of every past and future decision of the FCC with regard to programming. But the Court felt that Congress and the Federal Communications Commission do not violate the First Amendment when they require a radio or television station to give reply time to answer personal attacks and political editorials.

Broadcasters have claimed that the fairness doctrine does inhibit stations from covering controversial issues, and many have argued for its abolition. They have found some sympathy in Congress.

The 1960s witnessed a changing relationship between the courts and the Commission. While it is difficult to determine the extent to which Judge Burger's words in the *WLBT* case influenced the Commission, by the 1970s it was more likely to refuse to renew licenses than it was a few decades earlier. In fact, the Commission sent shock waves throughout the broadcasting industry when it refused to renew the lucrative license of a television station in a major market.

THE 1970s

The 1970s saw a flurry of court-FCC activities, and particularly in 1977, the Court of Appeals demonstrated an active interest in communications issues and reversed the Commission on numerous occasions.

In the three cases discussed here, the Court of Appeals sustained the action of the Commission, and the Supreme Court refused to review the cases. But in two recent decisions, the Commission was reversed by the Court of Appeals, and at least one of those cases, the *NBC* case, sparked a raging controversy over the way the fairness doctrine was applied to a network documentary.

A television license in a market the size of Boston can be tremendously profitable. When WHDH, Channel 5 in Boston, lost its license after a sixteen-year struggle to determine who should operate the station, it sent chills up and down the spine of the broadcasting industry. The *WHDH* case marks one of the few times a major television station has lost its license.

What is important about the case is that the U.S. Court of Appeals for the District of Columbia was satisfied with the process by which the Commission had made its decision, and even though individual members of the court might have decided differently under similar circumstances, the court would not disturb the FCC's decision.[27]

The *WHDH* case had been before the Court of Appeals three times before it finally affirmed the Commission's judgment. The court therefore had an unusual opportunity to examine the processes followed by the Commission in handling this particular case.

The issues are complex and recounting them unnecessary, but it is worthwhile to mention why the license was awarded to another applicant and to examine the court's comments on the process by which the Commission had made its decision.

The initial proceeding before the Commission to select a licensee to operate Channel 5 in Boston began in 1954 with considerations of four mutually exclusive applications. Three years later, the Commission granted the license to WHDH, Inc., a wholly owned subsidiary of the corporate publisher of the *Boston Herald-Traveler*.[28] The station began broadcasting the same year.

While the decision to award the license to WHDH, Inc., was on appeal to the U.S. Court of Appeals for the District of Columbia, the court was informed that the Commission's award of the license might have been subject to "an infirmity by virtue of improper *ex parte* contacts with the Chairman of the Commission."[29]

During the initial license proceedings, Robert Choate of WHDH had arranged two luncheons with George C. Mc-Connaughey, chairman of the Federal Communications Commission. The second lunch, in fact, took place in the spring of

1956, after the initial Hearing Examiner's decision favoring another applicant, but before oral argument before the Commission which reversed the Hearing Examiner.[30] Choate later claimed he arranged the meeting to discuss pending legislation in Congress and not his application before the Commission, but both the Commission and the Court of Appeals concluded that he "was sizing up the Chairman." The Commission discerned "a meaningful and improper, albeit subtle, attempt to influence the Commission, and condemned it as an effort that 'does violence to the integrity of the Commission's process.' "[31]

In the court's opinion, written by Judge Harold Leventhal, much attention was devoted to the scope of judicial review. Judge Leventhal cited what amounts to a "checklist" of procedures that the Commission must follow before receiving the court's "process approval." They included:

1. A requirement of reasonable procedure, with fair notice and opportunity to the parties to present their case.[32]
2. The court must be satisfied that the agency's fact findings are supported by substantial evidence and provide rational support for the agency's inferences of ultimate fact.[33]
3. The court must be satisfied that the agency has exercised a reasoned discretion, and with reasons that do not deviate from or ignore the ascertainable legislative intent.[34]
4. The court, because of its supervisory function, intervenes not merely in cases of procedural inadequacies or of bypassing the legislative mandate, but more broadly if the agency has not really taken a "hard look" at the salient problems and has not genuinely engaged in reasoned decision making.[35]
5. If the agency has not shirked the above-mentioned fundamental task, however, the court exercises restraint and affirms the agency's action even though the court would have made different findings or adopted different standards. Nor will the court upset a decision because of errors that are not material, there being room for the doctrine of harmless error.[36]
6. If satisfied that the agency has evaluated the issues using discernible reasons and standards, the court will uphold its findings, although of less than ideal clarity.[37]

Judge Leventhal understood that the requirement of "reasoned decision-making" is under great tension when an agency is required to choose among two or more applicants "endowed with virtually equivalent qualifications."[38] Satisfied that the Commission followed the above procedures, the court unanimously affirmed the Commission's decision to take away WHDH's license.

In his opinion, Judge Leventhal raised an interesting First Amendment issue that appears absent from most discussions and cases dealing with licensing. When the Commission makes a licensing decision concerning a company that also owns a newspaper, there is the possibility that "TV proceedings may come to involve overview of newspaper operations."[39] Separate from the issues of diversity of ownership, discussed in chapter 1, First Amendment issues are raised when the Commission investigates the qualifications of applicants who primarily operate newspapers. It is not appropriate here to search for relevant examples, but Judge Leventhal's discussion of the issue is worth some thought. In the *WHDH* case, the court was satisfied that no effort was made to determine the "public service" record of the *Boston Herald-Traveler*.[40] Some may argue that a newspaper's record is relevant to considering a broadcasting license, but that controversy should be explored elsewhere.

While some Court of Appeals and Supreme Court decisions considered here have not been unanimous, it is reasonable to conclude that the two benches have generally agreed as to when circumstances warrant court intervention in Commission decisions and when the issues were not ripe or appropriate for judicial review. The Supreme Court has usually been unanimous in its decision not to grant certiorari, but it is rare for a justice to publish a written dissent from the decision not to hear a case.

While the differences of opinion on points of law in any given case may be striking between majority and minority judges, it is rare for judges to engage in a "public debate" even over important issues. Usually, differences in interpretation are couched in legal terminology, which disguises what might otherwise appear to be hostility among the members over particular statutory or constitutional mandates.

This concept of judicial "comity," or deference, was clearly absent from one of the most significant cases before the Commission and the Court of Appeals. According to one commissioner, "it was the first time that the FCC had refused to renew a station's license because of fairness doctrine violations."[41]

On March 17, 1965, over the objections of various religious and civic organizations, the FCC approved the sale of WXUR-AM and WXUR-FM, in Media, Pennsylvania, to the Reverend Carl McIntire.[42] Offended by McIntire's broadcasts on another radio station in Chester, Pennsylvania, such groups as the National Council of Churches, the Urban League, and others asked the Commission to deny the transfer because of McIntire's history of "intemperate attacks on other religious denominations, various organizations, government agencies, and political figures."[43]

The Commission approved the transfer, but the approval was short lived. One year later, McIntire filed for a routine three-year license renewal. Once again, the same Philadelphia organizations protested, but this time they had more specific instances of WXUR and McIntire's "onesided, unbalanced, and weighted on the extreme right radicalism" broadcast in its first year of operation.[44]

Some of the offensive material was broadcast during WXUR's call-in show, presided over by Tom Livezey, a man described as possessing "a special talent for attracting those citizens of the City of Brotherly Love who stayed up late worrying about Jews, blacks, radicals, and Billy Graham."

Fred Friendly provides an example:

WOMAN LISTENER: About this B'nai B'rith Anti-Defamation League . . . why don't they get upset at all these smut and filth that's going through the mails?

LIVEZEY: And who do you think is behind all this obscenity that daily floods our mails, my dear?

LISTENER: Well, frankly, Tom, I think it is the Jewish people.

LIVEZEY: You bet your life it is.[45]

On another occasion Livezey encouraged a listener to read a poem about his desire to be a dog so that he could desecrate the grave of Franklin D. Roosevelt.[46]

Despite the protests, a hearing examiner determined that WXUR should keep its license. He concluded that "religion was underserved in the area . . . especially . . . conservative fundamentalist religion."[47] He also noted that the "entire broadcasting format over the license period and since has been one which welcomed all opposing viewpoints."[48]

In spite of the hearing examiner's determination, the Commission did not renew the license. And its explanation was extremely important because it caused serious disagreement among the judges of the Court of Appeals over the question of whether the license was taken away because of actual fairness doctrine violations or because of "misrepresentations" by the station as to how the fairness doctrine obligations were being met.

Judge Tamm, writing for a then unanimous three-judge panel of the Court of Appeals in *Brandywine-Main Line Radio v. Federal Communications Commission*,[49] questioned the station's dedication to the principles of the fairness doctrine:

The record of Brandywine-Main Line Radio is bleak in the area of good faith. At best, Brandywine's record is indicative of a lack of regard for fairness principles; at worst, it shows an utter disdain for Commission rulings and ignores its own responsibilities as a broadcaster and its representations to the Commission. . . . During the entire license period Brandywine willfully chose to disregard the Commission mandate.[50]

Referring to Brandywine's initial license application, the court said:

These men, with their hearts bent toward deliberate and premeditated deception, cannot be said to have dealt fairly with the Commission or the people in the Philadelphia area. Their statements constitute a series of heinous misrepresentations which, even without the other factors in this case, would be ample justification for the Commission to refuse to renew the broadcast license.[51]

Tucked away in the court's opinion were words of Chief Judge David Bazelon that were to have major significance forty days later. Judge Bazelon concurred "in affirming the decision of the FCC solely on the ground that the licensee deliberately withheld information about its programming plans."[52] But he added that a "full statement of his [Bazelon's] views will issue at a later date."[53]

When Judge Bazelon released the full statement on November 4, 1972, it reversed his previous position. He concluded that:

In this case I am faced with a *prima facie* violation of the First Amendment. The Federal Communications Commission has subjected Brandywine to the supreme penalty: it may no longer operate as a radio broadcast station. In silencing WXUR, the Commission has dealt a death blow to the licensee's freedoms of speech and press. Furthermore, it has denied the listening public access to the expression of many controversial views. Yet, the Commission would have us approve this action in the name of the fairness doctrine, the constitutional validity of which is premised on the argument that its enforcement will *enhance*[54] public access to a marketplace of ideas without serious infringement of the First Amendment rights of individual broadcasters.[55]

Judge Bazelon's detailed opinion, spanning seventeen pages, discussed the history of the First Amendment and the role of the press in American society. It concluded:

I originally authorized issuance of the opinions of the court with my concurrence resting on the narrow ledge of Brandywine's misrepresentations under the Supreme Court's ruling in *FCC v. WOKO, Inc.* But it is abundantly clear that the fairness doctrine is the "central aspect" of this case . . . I have therefore concluded that the great weight of First Amendment considerations cannot rest on so narrow a ledge.[56]

Judge Bazelon then explained how his second opinion could be so different from his first:

The point to be made is simply that I had originally thought that the alleged misrepresentation could be considered separately from the other issues in the case. But upon closer consideration, it became clear to me that the subject matter of the so-called deception is inextricably bound up in the considerations underlying the fairness doctrine.[57]

He expressed his gratitude to Justice Jackson, who provided some precedent for changing one's mind when he quoted Baron Bramwell as saying, "The matter does not appear to me now as it appears to have appeared to me then."[58]

The two judges concurring in the case, J. Skelly Wright and Edward Tamm, took issue with his conclusions and stated that Judge Bazelon's dissent seems to be an attack on the fairness doctrine; in fairness to the reader he should make clear at the outset of his opinion that the court's judgment in this case is not based on the fairness doctrine.[59]

Judge Wright then reiterated his position that WXUR's license was taken away because of misrepresentations about the fairness doctrine, not violations of the doctrine itself. According to Judge Wright, the Commission's judgment was based on two grounds:

1. Alleged violations of the fairness doctrine, and
2. Deception and misrepresentations made to the Commission by the licensee in obtaining the license.

Judge Bazelon stated in his dissent that he originally concurred in affirming the Commission because of the deception and mis-representations of the appellant but that Judge Wright is confused as to why he now dismisses that ground as "too narrow a ledge" on which to rest the Commission's action.[60]

Judge Wright then reminded Judge Bazelon that he rested his concurrence in the court's judgment *solely*[61] on the deception ground. "Since Judge Tamm would affirm the Commission on that ground also, that ground, and that ground alone, forms the basis of our judgment."[62]

Finally, Judge Wright concluded that the decision of the court did not reach the issue of the constitutionality of the fairness doctrine:

I do not think that deception in obtaining a government license is too narrow a ledge for voiding that license. The Supreme Court flatly so held in *FCC v. WOKO*, and there are no cases holding otherwise.[63]

What is missing from the opinions of Judges Wright and Tamm, and is mentioned only indirectly by Judge Bazelon, is that any applicant for a license automatically promises the Commission that he will abide by the provisions of the fairness doctrine when operating a broadcasting station. If such a commitment is not made, the license would be awarded to another applicant. It is unclear, therefore, whether a station is being punished for deceiving the Commission at the initial hearing when it promised to fulfill its fairness doctrine obligations or for actually violating the doctrine. Apparently, Judges Tamm and Wright feel more comfortable taking away a license because of deception, particularly since the Supreme

Court spoke so clearly on the subject in the *WOKO* case. To them, fewer constitutional issues are then raised. But Judge Bazelon is aware that this interpretation does not hide a more significant issue: Can the federal government stamp out and forever silence those whose broadcasts it finds distasteful and one-sided? Is it not possible, as Judge Bazelon questions, that applying the fairness doctrine in this case is ironic because it does silence different ideas, the very purpose the doctrine was supposed to serve?

Despite these problems, the FCC and a majority of a three-judge panel of the U.S. Court of Appeals applied the ultimate sanction to WXUR. The Supreme Court, with only Justice Douglas dissenting, refused to grant certiorari.[64]

A year later, the Court of Appeals again demonstrated that it would refrain from interfering in an FCC decision if the Commission had followed certain procedures. But unlike previous cases, the court did not hesitate to express its agreement, not only with the procedures followed in the case, but also with the outcome of the case.

The case was *Yale Broadcasting Company v. Federal Communications Commission*.[65] The source of the controversy was notice and orders issued by the Commission in March and April 1971 regarding "drug-oriented" music played by radio stations. Specifically, the Commission was concerned that the playing of songs with certain lyrics that glorified the use of drugs would encourage their use.

The FCC's initial order, in March 1971, was interpreted by many as prohibiting the playing of drug-related songs by licensees. Five weeks later, the Commission's Bureau of Complaints and Compliance provided broadcasters with the names of twenty-two songs labeled "drug oriented" on the basis of their lyrics.[66]

In April 1971, the Commission denied a petition to reconsider its April order but attempted to clarify its previous position. Although the Commission repudiated the list of banned songs, it reiterated the basic threat by noting that the "broadcaster could jeopardize his license by failing to exercise licensee responsibility in this area."[67]

The Yale Broadcasting Company challenged the rules on several grounds: that the Commission's action imposes an unconstitutional burden on a broadcaster's freedom of speech;[68] that the Commission's action was actually rule making and should have followed public hearings and other proceedings;[69] and that the Commission's order was impermissibly vague.[70]

A unanimous three-judge panel of the U.S. Court of Appeals for the District of Columbia rejected all three arguments and held not only that the Commission was within its statutory power to issue such regulations but also that to have not taken such action would have been a Commission failure to exercise its responsibility to ensure that broadcasting is regulated in the public interest.

Judge Malcolm Wilkey was clearly annoyed that the case came before the court, and at one point, he criticized the appellant for not understanding the Commission's order and for adding to the congestion of the federal courts:

> In spite of the horrendous forebodings which brought appellant into court the fact is that appellant has recently had its license renewed. Likewise, there has been no showing or suggestion that the standard enunciated in the Order has been employed to deny any license to a broadcaster. . . . Until that time, appellant might commit its energies to the simple task of understanding what the Commission has already clearly said, rather than instituting more colorful but far less fruitful actions before already heavily burdened federal courts.[71]

Judge Wilkey also dismissed Yale Broadcasting's claims that the Commission's rules violated freedom of speech provisions of the First Amendment. To Judge Wilkey, the key issue was whether licensees were responsible for what was played on their stations. Appellants attempted to persuade the court that the issues were similar to the *Smith v. California*[72] case, in which the Supreme Court held that a bookseller convicted of possessing and selling obscene literature had been unconstitutionally held responsible for the contents of the books.

Judge Wilkey considered the analogy specious. Because radio stations broadcast for a finite period of twenty-four hours each day, responsible station executives are able to monitor carefully their programming, an impossible task for the bookseller, whose store may contain many hours' worth of reading material.[73] In addition, Judge Wilkey interpreted the Commission's order to mean that a broadcaster does not have to prescreen everything but must be aware of what his station is broadcasting:

In order for a broadcaster to determine whether [he] is acting in the public interest, knowledge of his own programming is required. . . . We say that the licensee must have *knowledge* of what [he] is broadcasting; the precise *understanding* which may be required of the licensee is only that which is reasonable.[74]

Judge Wilkey held that to the extent lyrics are ambiguous the Commission allows the licensee discretion in determining whether they should be banned. He felt that since some lyrics are virtually "unintelligible, to the extent they are completely meaningless gibberish and approach the equivalent of machinery operating or the din of traffic," they are not within the ambit of the Commission's order.[75]

The court also dismissed appellant's argument that the Commission's action was rule making and therefore not promulgated under proper procedures. The court concluded that the Commission was imposing no new duty on broadcasters but was merely reminding them of their preexisting duty to serve in the public interest.[76]

Finally, appellants argued that because they had submitted a six-page written statement as to how they planned to comply with the new rules, and the Commission had refused to issue a declaratory judgment on the acceptability of the proposed plan, the Commission was abusing the discretion granted to it to promulgate rules and procedures. Judge Wilkey dismissed the contention that the Commission was required to issue such a declaratory statement:

There are over 7,500 radio stations in this country. If the Commission were required to pass upon, approve, or disapprove, the methods of operations of each of these stations, the administrative task would be enormous. This disinclination to rule here is in accord with the Commission's long standing policy of refusing to issue interpretative rulings or advisory opinions whenever the critical facts are not explicitly stated or there is a possibility that subsequent events will alter them.[77]

The panel that heard the *Yale* case consisted of Judges John Danaher, Spottswood Robinson, and Malcolm Wilkey. Chief Judge Bazelon was concerned that the decision of the court did not properly consider the First Amendment rights of free speech, and he offered a motion for rehearing *en banc*, which was rejected.

In his dissent to denial of the motion for a rehearing, Judge Bazelon contended that the Commission's action, whether intended or not, resulted in banning from the airwaves twenty-two songs of which the Commission disapproved. Judge Bazelon had serious concerns over whether such an action constituted censorship.[78] He concluded that the Commission's second order, attempting to clarify its March opinion, resulted in an even more direct threat against broadcasters in that if they continued to play such music they risked losing their licenses.

Judge Bazelon quoted FCC Chairman Dean Burch before a Senate Committee:

CHAIRMAN BURCH: Contrary to Commissioner Johnson's statement that we banned drug lyrics, we did not ban drug lyrics. . . .

Moments later, however, the following ensued:

SENATOR NELSON: All I am asking is: If somebody calls to the FCC's attention that a particular station is playing songs that, in fact, do promote the use of drugs in the unanimous judgment of the Commission, if you came to that conclusion, what would you do?

CHAIRMAN BURCH: I know what I would do, I probably would vote to take the license away.[79]

In discussing the scope of judicial review, Judge Bazelon acknowledged that the court should grant wide discretion to the Commission in "actions in technical areas—e.g. policing broadcasters' mechanical operations and interference between stations—. . . but no such deference is due in cases involving the Commission's 'public interest' regulation of program content." To Judge Bazelon, "courts have a special responsibility to protect First Amendment rights and a special expertise for doing so."[80]

The court must be concerned not just with the directives themselves but also with the impact of the directives. In other words, Judge Bazelon recognized that the threat of legal action can have as much effect on conduct as the sanction itself. The court, according to Judge Bazelon, must consider whether the effect of the

Commission's order is self-censorship, which the court cannot tolerate.

Finally, Judge Bazelon wondered whether a popular song is a constitutionally protected form of speech and whether songs with certain lyrics do, in fact, encourage drug use. He had hoped the court would have dealt with those key issues.

On October 15, 1973, the Supreme Court, with Justices Douglas and William Brennan dissenting, refused to grant certiorari.[81] Justice Douglas wrote a dissent tracing the events leading up to the Court of Appeals decision and urging the Supreme Court to consider the case. He reiterated his view that "TV and radio stand in the same protected position under the First Amendment as do newspapers and magazines."[82] Since no one would seriously consider that, consistent with the First Amendment, the government could force a newspaper out of business if its news stories betrayed too much sympathy with those arrested on marijuana charges, Justice Douglas concluded, the Commission places unconstitutional burdens on broadcasters:

> The Commission imposes on the licensees a responsibility to analyze the meaning of each song's lyrics and make a judgment as to the social value of the message. The message may be clear or obscure, and careful scrutiny would seem required. This task is to be carried out under the Commission's watchful eye and with the knowledge that repeated errors will be punished by revocation of the license.[83]

To Justice Douglas, the same margin of error that was allowed print journalists in *New York Times v. Sullivan*[84] should be granted to broadcasters: "Songs play no less a role in public debate . . . and the Government cannot, consistent with the First Amendment, require broadcasters to censor its music any more than it can require newspapers to censor the stories of its reporters. Under our system the Government is not to decide what messages, spoken or in music, are of the proper 'social value' to reach the people."[85]

THE PENSIONS CASE

Few cases ever presented the Court of Appeals with as many difficult issues as that of the *National Broadcasting Company v. Federal Communications Commission*.[86] While a number of the cases discussed in chapters 2 and 3 involved enforcement of provisions of the fairness doctrine, no other case so severely tested the appropriateness and constitutionality of government-imposed "fairness," and none has dealt with a television network documentary.

On September 12, 1972, the NBC Television Network broadcast *Pensions: The Broken Promise,* narrated by correspondent Edwin Newman. By the time the Court of Appeals issued its final opinion, nearly three years later, the issues had not only alarmed the broadcasting industry but also had badly splintered the court, obscuring any clear statement of judicial ideology on certain key communications issues.

The program dealt with abuses in the private pension plan system and concluded that paying into a pension plan for years was no guarantee that an individual would receive benefits. The broadcast centered on interviews with a number of aging workers who described, often in moving detail, their firsthand experiences with pension plan abuse.[87]

On November 27, 1972, a group called Accuracy in Media (AIM) filed a complaint with the Federal Communications Commission charging that NBC had presented a one-sided picture of private pension plans and had violated the fairness doctrine by failing to afford reasonable opportunity to present contrasting views.

Although it is not appropriate here to discuss in detail the documentary, one does get the impression from reading a transcript that NBC was highly critical of private pension plans and that relatively little was said on the positive side. NBC claimed that it was unsuccessful in its attempts to interview individuals who would praise pension plans.

At the end of the broadcast, Newman summed up their findings, beginning with a disclaimer that was to become the subject of much legal discussion:

This is a depressing program to work on, but we don't want to give the impression that there are no good private pension plans. There are many good ones, and there are many people for whom the promise has become a reality. That should be said.[88]

Then Newman urged individuals enrolled in private pension plans to take a close look at their own situation, and he ended by saying:

Our own conclusion about all of this is that it is almost inconceivable that this enormous thing has been allowed to grow up with so little under-standing of it and with so little protection and such uneven results for those involved. The situation, as we've seen it, is deplorable. Edwin Newman, NBC News.[89]

AIM demanded that NBC grant it time to reply to the impression that private pension plans were often not what people expected them to be. Accuracy in Media itself will be discussed later. For now, it is appropriate to note that AIM, a "third party," was the vehicle by which the issues were brought to the Commission and the Court of Appeals.

On the same day that NBC was awarded the George Foster Peabody Award for *Pensions*,[90] the Commission staff decided that NBC had indeed violated the fairness doctrine and would have twenty days to describe to the Commission what "counter-programming" it intended to broadcast to show the "other side." NBC refused to comply with the Commission when it approved its staff recommendation, and NBC appealed to the Court of Appeals.

The *Pensions* case presented the court with many complex issues. The Commission had ruled that a network documentary had violated the fairness doctrine and that the network must provide reply time. Unlike Reverend Billy James Hargis and the *Red Lion* case, NBC claimed it made a reasonable effort to obtain interviews with articulate defenders of the pension system. In the *Red Lion* case, it will be recalled, Hargis' purpose was to attack Fred J. Cook, and Red Lion Broadcasting Company refused to provide reply time.

But the *Pensions* case presented different issues. The former president of NBC News, Reuven Frank, summed up well the broad-caster's point of view:

The "Pensions" program was put together by a group of reporters and editors who had no stake in how it came out, except to tell people more than they might already know about something of interest to them. . . . The reply, if there were to be one, would necessarily be by someone who had a position to promote, one identifiable in advance. Then his credentials would be presented as journalistically equal to those of the reporters and editors who did the program.[91]

Frank then distinguished journalism from discussion:

Journalism is a recognizable sort of activity, certainly to other journalists. So long as it is confused with discussion, we're going to have a rhetorical muddle. . . . The "Pensions" program was not a discussion; it was a job of reporting. Having it subject to reply as though it were one side of a discussion damages journalism. Debating is not the journalist's job; reporting is. [92]

Another difference between the *Red Lion* and *Pensions* cases, although somewhat less important, was that Cook himself asked for reply time. In the *Pensions* case, a third party, AIM, asked for time as a "watchdog" of the media, not as a representative of individuals operating pension plans.

On December 3, 1973, Commission Chairman Dean Burch and four of his colleagues upheld the May 2 staff report. While commending NBC for a laudable journalistic effort, the FCC found that the network had not satisfied its fairness obligations and ordered it to do so immediately. The Commission agreed with AIM that the "overwhelming weight" of the antipension statements required further presentation of opposing views.[93]

NBC could have satisfied the Commission's order in any number of ways, but refused to do so. In the words of one veteran NBC newsman not connected with the documentary:

To be found guilty of "unfairness" for not expressing to the government's satisfaction the view that most people are not corrupt or that pensioners are not unhappy is to be judged by standards which simply have nothing to do with journalism.[94]

The Commission demanded that, while the case was being considered by the courts, NBC fulfill its fairness obligations. Again, the network refused to comply until the courts heard the case. NBC's lawyer, Floyd Abrams, argued that "compulsive government programming against the will of the licensee *prior* to judicial review cannot be undone by an after-the-fact reversal of the Commission's decision in this case."[95] In the case before the Court of Appeals, CBS, the Radio and Television News Directors Association, the National Association of Broadcasters, and *The New York Times* filed amicus briefs on NBC's side.

To the surprise of many, former FCC general counsel Henry Geller also submitted a brief that argued that, if there were fairness violations, they could be considered only at the end of the licensing period, when assessing the licensee's overall record.[96]

Judge Harold Leventhal of the Court of Appeals believed that because Congress was currently examining the abuses of private pension plans raised by the NBC documentary an immediate hearing was necessary. Suggesting a most unusual judicial procedure, he asked NBC and the FCC to eliminate the preparation of lengthy briefs and to argue the case in court as soon as possible.

The court heard the case on February 21, 1974. NBC argued before the three-judge panel that its discretion had been overruled by the Commission in a way that neither the fairness doctrine nor the First Amendment would allow. Judge Leventhal was particularly concerned after being told by NBC that no one at AIM or the Commission had ever seen a video tape of the documentary, only written transcripts. Among other things, NBC claimed that since television is a visual medium a program cannot be judged by reading transcripts of dialogue.

The Commission's lawyer, John Pettit, argued that as Congress, the courts, and the Commission had stated, the rights of the viewers and listeners are paramount, not the rights of the broadcasters.

Judge Charles Fahy asked Pettit about Newman's concluding statement, which acknowledged that there were many good plans. Pettit replied that Newman's conclusion did not correct the program's basically negative attitude and that NBC's refusal to schedule a rebuttal was a dereliction of its fairness responsibilities.

When the court issued its opinion, on September 27, 1974, two of the three judges agreed with NBC that the Commission had exceeded its authority and had placed a government body in the position of second-guessing editors. Judge Leventhal, writing for himself and Judge Fahy, reversed the Commission's decision as a misapplication of the fairness doctrine. Because the court reversed on that ground, wrote Judge Leventhal, there had been no occasion to consider the First Amendment issues.[97]

Judge Leventhal held that the Commission was unable to prove that the "licensee had failed to provide reasonable opportunity for the presentation of contrasting approaches."[98] He then turned to the key issue:

The Court has sustained the fairness doctrine in broadcasting as an instance of a necessary control in the public interest. The broadcaster cannot assert a right of freedom of press that transcends the public's right to know. But application of the fairness doctrine must still recognize the enduring values of wide latitude of journalistic discretion in the licensee. And when a court is called on to take a "hard look" whether the Commission has gone too far and encroached on journalistic discretion, it must take a hard look to avoid enforcing judicial predilections.[99]

The court understood that when dealing with investigative journalism there is the greatest need for self-restraint on the part of the Commission since "investigative journalism is a portrayal of evils."[100]

Judge Tamm bitterly dissented on the grounds that the court's majority had rendered the fairness doctrine virtually unenforceable. He claimed that the tremendous power of the broadcasting industry required careful government scrutiny and repeated his long-held belief that the fairness doctrine is not censorship.

In the months following the decision, it became clear that Judge Leventhal's colleagues on the bench were unhappy with his decision, and rumors circulated that if the Commission or AIM asked for a rehearing *en banc* such a request would be granted. The Commission did not make such a request, but AIM petitioned the court and was granted a hearing. On December 13, 1974, the court approved the petition and vacated Judge Leventhal's opinion, although the court sustained his order staying the Commission's order to NBC until the *en banc* judgment was rendered.

The court ordered that written briefs be delivered within forty days. Oral arguments were to be heard on April 2, 1975. But *en banc* arguments never took place. Two weeks before the case was to be heard, a majority of the judges decided that they did not wish to hear the case. Judge Bazelon had been anxious for the *en banc* arguments to proceed, for he was hoping that he could persuade enough of his colleagues that the time was right to consider the constitutionality of the fairness doctrine itself. Apparently, the Commission, which had never been happy with the *Pensions* case as a test of the fairness doctrine, convinced enough members of the court that, since Congress had passed the Employment Retirement Income Security Act of 1974, there was no longer a need to debate an issue that Congress had already decided.

With the vacating of the *en banc* hearing, the case was remanded to

Judge Leventhal's three-judge panel so that it could rule on the mootness question or reaffirm the original opinion in favor of NBC.

Judge Bazelon did not wait for the panel to make a decision. In June 1975, he issued a blistering attack against the eight judges who had vacated the *en banc* hearing, claiming that the courts had thereby further confused the issues surrounding the fairness doctrine. Judge Bazelon was particularly critical of NBC's counsel's position that the documentary had not dealt with controversial issues of public importance:

I wonder what the professional journalists who prepared the "Pensions" program think about NBC's litigation position in this case that their program was not really controversial. My own thought is that NBC has by its litigation position done more to attack and undercut the "Pensions" program than anything AIM could have done through the FCC. This is the saddest commentary of all.[101]

Six weeks later, Judges Leventhal and Fahy agreed to remand the case to the Commission, which had said it would drop all proceedings. Judge Fahy spoke to the mootness issue:

The Commission seeks the remand on the theory of mootness. It is clear, however, that this theory is simply the medium advanced by the Commission to enable the case to be ended without a definitive decision on the merits. The essence of the matter is that the Commission seeks permission to vacate its order.[102]

This was a strange ending to one of the most important broadcasting cases. The broadcasters, and many concerned about the constitutionality and application of the fairness doctrine, hope that the decision by Leventhal and Fahy will not be forgotten. The Supreme Court agreed to lay the matter to rest temporarily by denying certiorari.

Although broadcasters had won a moral victory, it did not have the force of law and probably cannot be cited as precedent. The *Pensions* case, however, does clearly demonstrate the difficulty the courts have in reviewing Commission decisions imposing government standards of "fairness."

THE PACIFICA CASE

The last case to be discussed in this chapter raised some significant issues, but because of the subject matter, it may have limited application in future cases. *Federal Communications Commission v. Pacifica Foundation*[103] did demonstrate, however, that the Supreme Court will intervene when it deems that the Court of Appeals inappropriately limits the Commission's discretion in interpreting the public interest standard.

At 2 PM on Tuesday, October 30, 1973, radio station WBAI-FM, owned by Pacifica Foundation, broadcast a monologue by comedian George Carlin entitled "Filthy Words." A tape of a live show that Carlin did before a California audience, he introduced the monologue by saying that these were words you could not say on the public airwaves. He turned out to be right.

A few weeks later, a man who heard the broadcast while driving with his young son in New York City, complained to the Commission that his son should not have been exposed to such a program. The Commission forwarded the complaint to Pacifica, which said that the monologue had been part of a program about society's attitude toward language and that listeners had been advised that it included "sensitive language which might be regarded as offensive to some."[104]

In its response, Pacifica characterized Carlin as:

a significant social satirist who like Twain and Sahl before him, examines the language of ordinary people . . . Carlin is not mouthing obscenities, he is merely using words to satirize as harmless and essentially silly our attitudes towards those words.[105]

Pacifica also claimed that it had received no other complaints about the broadcast.

On February 21, 1975, the Commission issued a Declaratory Order granting the complaint and holding that Pacifica could be the subject of administrative sanctions.[106] The Commission did not impose formal sanctions, but it did state that the order would be

associated with the station's license file, and in the event that subsequent complaints are received, the Commission will then decide whether it should utilize any of the available sanctions it has been granted by Congress.[107]

It was generally agreed that the Carlin monologue lacked the "prurient interest" characteristics necessary to be considered obscene, but the Commission held that it had the statutory authority to regulate indecent as well as obscene language. The Commission found such authority in two statutes: 18 U.S.C. Section 1464, which stated "Whoever utters any obscene, indecent or profane language by means of radio communications shall be fined not more than $10,000 or imprisoned not more than two years, or both"; and 47 U.S.C. Section 303 (g), which requires the Commission to "encourage the larger and more effective use of radio in the public interest."

The Commission characterized the language used by Carlin as "patently offensive," although not necessarily obscene. The Commission held that the concept of *indecent* is intimately connected with the exposure of children to language that "describes in terms patently offensive as measured by contemporary community standards *for the broadcast medium*,[108] sexual or excretory activities and organs, at times of the day when there is a reasonable risk that children may be in the audience."[109]

After the order was issued, the Commission clarified its opinion by ruling that the broadcast of indecent words as part of a live newscast would not be prohibited. It stated that it "never intended to place an absolute prohibition on the broadcast of this type of language, but rather sought to channel it to times of day when children most likely would not be exposed to it."[110]

The Court of Appeals reversed the Commission on a 2-1 vote,[111] with an unusual lineup of judges. Judge Tamm, often critical of broadcasting, concluded that the Commission's order was censorship within the meaning of Section 326 of the Communications Act.[112] In addition, he concluded that the Commission's opinion was the functional equivalent of a rule and as such that it was "overbroad."

Chief Judge Bazelon's concurrence rested on constitutional grounds. He concluded that Section 326's prohibition against censorship was inapplicable to broadcasts forbidden by Section 1464. However, he held that Section 1464 must be narrowly construed to cover language that is obscene or otherwise unprotected by the First Amendment. Judge Leventhal, who had been sympathetic to broadcasters' claims in the *Pensions* case, dissented. Emphasizing the interest in protecting children from exposure not only to indecent language but also to the idea that such language has official approval, he concluded that the Commission had correctly condemned the daytime broadcast as indecent.

The Supreme Court reversed by a 5-4 decision. Justice John Paul Stevens, writing for the majority, held that the Commission was warranted in concluding that indecent language was within the meaning of Section 1464 and that it could ban indecent, although not obscene, language. The Commission has the right, Justice Stevens held, to sanction licensees who engage in such practices.

Justice Stevens then stated what a number of courts had held over the years; namely, that of all forms of communication, broadcasting has the most limited First Amendment protection:

> The reasons for these distinctions are complex, but two have relevance to the present case. First, the broadcast media have established a uniquely pervasive presence in the lives of all Americans. Patently offensive, indecent material presented over the airwaves confronts the citizen, not only in public, but also in the privacy of the home, where the individual's right to be let alone plainly outweighs the First Amendment rights of an intruder.[113]

Justice Stevens also said that because the broadcast audience is constantly tuning in and out prior warnings cannot completely protect it against "unexpected program content." He also concluded that since broadcasting is uniquely available to children the Commission was correct in preventing them from being exposed to such programs.

Justice Brennan, dissenting, held that the word "indecent" in Section 1464 must be construed to prohibit only obscene speech. He found the "Court's misapplication of fundamental First Amendment principles so patent, and its attempt to impose *its*[114] notions of propriety on the whole of the American people so misguided, that I am unable to remain silent."[115]

He agreed with Justice Stevens that an individual was entitled to be "let alone" in the privacy of his own home. However, Justice Brennan believed

> that an individual's actions in switching on and listening to communications transmitted over the public airwaves and directed to the public at-large do not implicate fundamental privacy interests, even when engaged within the home.[116]

It was Justice Brennan's belief that an individual may choose not to partake or participate in an ongoing public discussion and that a decision to allow radio communications into his home does not abrogate all of his privacy interests. He understood parents' concern about what reaches their children, and he admitted a legitimate government interest in the well-being of children, but he was critical of the Court, which, "for the first time, allows the government to prevent minors from gaining access to materials that are not obscene, and are therefore protected."[117]

Even if the monologue appealed to the prurient interest of minors, it would not be obscene, according to Justice Brennan, unless it met the *Miller v. California* test that "the work, taken as a whole, lacks serious literary, artistic, political, or scientific value."[118]

CONCLUSION

Chapters 2 and 3 have examined a number of broadcasting cases in the federal courts that were chosen either because of the substantive issues raised or because they provided opportunities for jurists to comment on the role of courts in reviewing and influencing communications policy.

Two essential questions are raised by such a review. The first is one of measurement: What are the courts doing to influence communications policy? The second is normative: What is the proper role of the courts? While both questons have been blended together here, the second will be considered in more detail in chapter 4, on the political environment of the Federal Communications Commission.

Although broad statements about the role of courts are difficult to make, perhaps it can be accurately said that judicial intervention has been relatively consistent in a broad range of broadcasting issues. In addition, a majority of the cases have come to one particular court, the U.S. Court of Appeals for the District of Columbia, which has implications mentioned in chapter 2.

The courts have appeared to welcome their "activist" role. The Court of Appeals for the District of Columbia, for example, has relatively "liberal" rules of standing that have allowed participation by viewers and listeners who might not be able to establish standing under stricter standards. That has led to the court's involvement in a number of cases raising "public interest" issues, rather than just the concerns among the parties in the case. Technically, the Court of Appeals can review any Commission order that adversely affects someone's interests. The court has interpreted this power broadly to allow individuals to vindicate a more general public interest.

While the standing issue is important, the more significant question deals with what the courts have done when the cases arrive. The Court of Appeals' "activist" role has sparked debate over whether it has inappropriately crossed the boundary between judicial review and outright supervision of the Commission. It can be argued that when First Amendment issues are involved the courts are uniquely suited and responsible for closely monitoring how those principles are applied, and that a Commission of political appointees, with close ties to interest groups, Congress, and others, cannot be left alone to make important decisions affecting the First Amendment. On the other hand, others claim that courts have abused their special status and independence by venturing into areas historically reserved for other branches of government.

From examining these cases, it would be difficult to assert that courts have abused their special role in our society. In numerous cases, the courts have refused to interfere with Commission decisions on important issues. And on other occasions when the Court of Appeals has disturbed an FCC decision, the Supreme Court has intervened and restored the Commission's judgment.

Plaguing any analysis is the absence of any standard for measuring the relative importance of individual cases. Some have suggested that courts are more likely to affirm in minor cases than in those involving major policy issues. Such a conclusion, however, could not be drawn from the cases discussed here. Still, deciding which cases are important is clearly subjective. Even if one attempted to measure cases by their relationship to the First Amendment, all but the most insignificant cases would almost inevitably be included.

Glen O. Robinson, in a study of the role of courts in communications policy,[119] examined the results of a number of cases from two periods, 1950-1956 and 1970-1976. He concluded that judicial activity has increased in recent decades. The number of reported opinions in the 1970-1976 period is more than double that of the 1950-1956 period. Among other reasons, Robinson claimed that much of the increase is due to an increase in Commission activity in traditional areas (as opposed to cable television, for example) and to an increase in litigation by public interest groups that were virtually unrepresented in the 1950-1956 period.

Judicial review of communications decisions has made administrative decision making more visible and has provided means for challenging it. While courts themselves may be no more "accountable" than administrative agencies, some individuals who find it difficult to get the attention of the commissioners of the FCC undoubtedly have found the courts willing to listen. Such an arrangement may foster greater participation and a greater degree of "democratic responsibility" in the administrative decision-making process.

Additional evidence of increased judicial activism in communications cases is that during 1977, a period not covered by Robinson, more than half of all appeals of FCC decisions to the Court of Appeals for the District of Columbia resulted in a reversal of some significant part of the FCC's decision.[120]

NOTES

1. A 1964 case should be mentioned briefly. In *E. G. Robinson v. Federal Communications Commission*, 334 F.2d 534, the Commission refused to renew the license of radio station WDKD, and a three-judge panel of the Court of Appeals unanimously affirmed the decision.

The case concerned a disc jockey who allegedly used program material that was "coarse, vulgar, suggestive, and susceptible of indecent, double meaning" (p. 535). The key issue in the Commission's decision was that the owner of the station had not taken care to monitor his facility and that he ignored complaints from listeners about the programs. The court determined also that the owner had misled the Commission as to whether he had been informed about complaints from listeners.

2. Fred W. Friendly, *The Good Guys, the Bad Guys and the First Amendment* (New York: Vintage Books, 1976), p. 90.

3. Ibid., p. 95.

4. Ibid., p. 96.

5. Ibid., p. 101.

6. See note 4, chapter 2.

7. 359 F.2d at 1002.

8. Ibid., p. 1003.

9. Steve Millard, "Broadcasting's Pre-Emptive Court," 81 *Broadcasting Magazine* (August 30, 1971): 23.

10. 359 F.2d at 1009.

11. Friendly, p. 99.

12. Ibid.

13. Ibid.

14. 425 F.2d at 549-50.

15. Ibid., p. 546.

16. Ibid., p. 550.

17. *Brandywine-Main Line Radio v. Federal Communications Commission,* 473 F.2d 16 (1972).

18. 395 U.S. 367 (1969).

19. Friendly, p. 5.

20. Ibid., p. 46.

21. 395 U.S. at 375.

22. Ibid., p. 380.

23. Ibid., p. 388.

24. Ibid., p. 390.

25. Ibid., p. 393.

26. Ibid., p. 391.

27. 444 F.2d 841.

28. Ibid., p. 844.

29. Ibid.

30. Ibid., pp. 844-45.

31. Ibid., p. 845.

32. Ibid., p. 850.

33. Ibid.

34. Ibid.

35. Ibid., p. 851.

36. Ibid.

37. Ibid.

38. Ibid., p. 852.

39. Ibid., p. 854.

40. Ibid., p. 855.

41. Commissioner Robert E. Lee, quoted in Friendly, p. 82.

42. Friendly, p. 80.

43. Ibid.

44. Ibid.

45. Ibid., p. 81.

46. Ibid.

47. Ibid., p. 82.

48. Ibid.

49. 473 F.2d 16.

50. Ibid., pp. 46-47.

51. Ibid., p. 52.

52. Ibid., p. 63.

53. Ibid.

54. His emphasis.

55. 473 F.2d at 63.

56. Ibid., p. 80.

57. Ibid.

58. Ibid.

59. Ibid.

60. Ibid., p. 81.

61. His emphasis.

62. 473 F.2d at 81.

63. Ibid.

64. Friendly, pp. 87-88.

65. 478 F.2d 594 (1973).

66. In its subsequent order in April, the Commission reported that the list of twenty-two songs had been identified by the Department of the Army. 414 U.S. at 914. (Cert. denied, Douglas dissenting).

67. Ibid., p. 915 (Douglas dissenting).

68. 478 F.2d at 597.

69. Ibid., p. 599.

70. Ibid., p. 601.

71. Ibid., p. 602.

72. 361 U.S. 147 (1959).

73. 478 F.2d at 598.

74. Ibid.

75. Ibid.

76. Ibid., p. 599.

77. Ibid., p. 602.

78. Ibid., p. 603.

79. Ibid., p. 604.

80. Ibid., pp. 604-05.

81. 414 U.S. 914.

82. Ibid., p. 916.

83. Ibid., p. 917.

84. 376 U.S. 254 (1964).

85. 414 U.S. at 918.

86. 516 F.2d 1101 (1974).

87. Friendly, p. 144.

88. Ibid., p. 145.

89. Ibid., p. 146.

90. Many consider the Peabody award to be "broadcasting's Pulitzer" and the industry's most prestigious award.

91. Reuven Frank, "A Fairness Doctrine for Journalists?" *The New York Times* (July 20, 1975), Letters to the Editor.

92. Ibid.

93. 40 F.C.C. 958 (May 2, 1973); 44 F.C.C. 1026 (January 29, 1974).

94. David Brinkley, quoted in Friendly, p. 153.

95. Friendly, p. 154.

96. Ibid., p. 153.

97. 516 F.2d at 1109.

98. Ibid., p. 1130.

99. Ibid., p. 1132.

100. Ibid., p. 1133.

101. Ibid., p. 1179.

102. Ibid., p. 1182.

103. 438 U.S. 726 (1978).

104. 438 U.S. at 730.

105. Ibid.

106. 56 F.C.C. 2d 94, 99 (1975).

107. 438 U.S. at 730.

108. My emphasis.

109. 56 F.C.C. 2d at 98.

110. 59 F.C.C. 2d 892 (1976).

111. 556 F.2d 9.

112. Section 326 states: "Nothing in this Act shall be understood or construed to give the Commission the power of censorship over the radio communications or signals transmitted by any radio station, and no regulation or condition shall be promulgated or fixed by the Commission which shall interfere with the right of free speech by means of radio communication." 48 Stat. 1091.

113. 438 U.S. at 748.

114. His emphasis.

115. 438 U.S. at 762.

116. 438 U.S. at 764-65.

117. 438 U.S. at 767.

118. 413 U.S. 15 (1973).

119. Glen O. Robinson. "The Judicial Role," *Communications for Tomorrow*, ed. Glen O. Robinson (New York: Praeger Publishers, 1978), pp. 415-44.

120. Ibid., p. 427.

4.

The Political Environment of the Federal Communications Commission

The Federal Communications Commissions is a creature of Congress, staffed at its highest levels by White House appointees, subject at every moment to judicial review, and faced with daily pressures from the industries it regulates, other branches of government, and the public whose interest it was created to protect.[1]

The FCC operates in a complex political environment. Because the Commission is charged with the weighty responsibility of regulating media of communication, it is particularly important to examine the environment in which broadcasting policy decisions are made. This chapter will discuss the major actors in that environment and their relationship to the Commission.

Evaluating the relative contributions of these various actors is complicated by the fact that the Commission's performance is judged by the "public interest" standard; yet the Communications Act of 1934 provides few clues as to what constitutes the public interest. The questions raised are many: What is the public interest? Which publics? Under what circumstances are the interests of certain publics served? (Appendix A provides an analytical model for evaluating these actors' relative contributions to FCC policymaking and will suggest issues that lend themselves to analysis to test the model.)

The Commission's environment contains many actors, but they form relatively clear patterns of behavior when interacting with the Commission. The FCC's environment contains what could be described as a "daily operating" constituency consisting of a group of actors with whom the Commission and its staff interact on a continuing, almost daily basis. A secondary constituency, on the other hand, is not involved in routine Commission decisions and is often activated only after a particularly important issue arises. There are exceptions, but for the most part, the secondary constituency merely "reacts" to Commission decisions and plays a relatively minor role in the policymaking process. Unlike the primary constituency, the secondary group does not follow the daily activities of the Commission and, after a particular issue or decision is resolved, will often turn away from FCC matters and focus on issues it then considers more salient.

The distinction between primary and secondary actors in the Commission's political environment is significant because it indicates a common problem of regulatory agencies: the agency has much greater contact with those whom it is supposed to regulate than with those in whose interest it is supposed to regulate.

Below is a partial list of key actors in the Commission's environment:

The FCC's primary constituency includes:

—Congress (particularly the communications subcommittees of the Senate Commerce Committee and the House Interstate and Foreign Commerce Committee)

—the White House (particularly staff concerned with patronage and domestic policy)

—interest/clientele groups (particularly the National Association of Broadcasters and multiple station owners)

—trade press (although its function is somewhat different from other actors)[2]

—some executive branch agencies (such as the National Telecommunications and Information Administration in the Commerce Department)

The FCC's secondary constituency includes:

—the public (including public interest groups, such as the National Citizens Committee for Broadcasting and the Parent-Teachers Association)

—other executive branch agencies (including the Federal Trade Commission, Office of Management and Budget, and the Justice Department)

—the judicial branch

—general media

This list does not include all possible primary and secondary actors but identifies the most influential ones in terms of policy-making. Any discussion of the political environment of the FCC must reflect an understanding of the system's dynamic aspects. Actors in the Commission's environment do not interact with the FCC independent of each other. For example, what action the communications committees in Congress take may depend on how members of the committees have been influenced by broadcasters or the general public. The Commission's dealings with the Federal Trade Commission or the Office of Management and Budget may be affected by White House or congressional intervention.

Any discussion of the FCC's environment must begin with the Commission itself. The FCC is more than a regulatory commission seeking to regulate the broadcasting industry; it is also a bureaucracy. As such, it exhibits many of the classic symptoms of bureaucracies—massive hierarchy, institutional conservatism, professed rationality, and entrenched self-interest.[3]

The Communications Act created the FCC with seven commissioners but said little about their qualifications. Technically, they are appointed by the President with the advice and consent of the Senate, but as will be seen shortly, Congress is very much involved in the nominating process, and few nominees encounter confirmation difficulties in the Senate.[4]

The commissioners are appointed to seven-year terms and may be reappointed by the President. The Act states that no more than four can be of the same political party and that they cannot hold financial interests in companies connected with the regulated industries. Section 4 of the Act, dealing with appointments and terminations, states that if a commissioner resigns before his term expires he must wait one year before representing an individual or company before the Commission. This rule does not apply if the term is completed. Section 4 also provides that the President designate one commissioner to serve as chairman and chief executive officer.

Other rules set forth in the Act state that four commissioners constitute a quorum and that general sessions open to the public be held once a month. The Commission is required to submit an annual report to Congress.

The Commission has undergone a number of staff reorganizations since its establishment in 1934. The staff was originally organized by specialized knowledge, consisting of three divisions, with three commissioners heading each division. Jurisdictional disputes developed among the commissioners, and differences in workload required some commissioners to assume more responsibility than others. Eventually, this arrangement proved unworkable. Because of the interrelationships among the telegraph, telephone, and broadcast industries, a commissioner's competency in one area of regulation was limited by his lack of experience and knowledge in others. Such a system was not conducive to cooperation and mutual understanding.[5]

On October 13, 1937, the telegraph, telephone, and broadcast divisions were abolished, and the full Commission assumed responsibility for their functions. Henceforth, each commissioner theoretically had an equal voice in all policy determinations and other matters.[6]

Despite these changes, by the late 1940s Congress became irritated by the time it took the Commission to process applications and to conduct other business. There was a mounting backload of work at the Commission. In 1952, Congress amended the Communications Act to reorganize the staff on a functional basis. Section 5 was amended to require the Commission, within six months, to organize the staff into ''(1) integrated bureaus, to function on the basis of the Commission's principal workload operations, and (2) make such other divisional organizations as the Commission may deem necessary.''[7] By the time Congress passed the 1952 amendments, the FCC, anticipating congressional action, had begun to reorganize itself along the lines informally suggested by Congress.

As a result of the 1952 amendments, the staff was and remains today organized into five bureaus and a number of staff offices, including among others the Broadcast Bureau, Common Carrier Bureau, Safety and Special Radio Services Bureau, Field Engineering Bureau, Cable TV Bureau, Office of Hearing Examiners (included as a result of the Administrative Procedure Act of 1946), and Office of Opinion and Review.

The FCC's middle staff is a significant factor in developing regulatory policy. Unlike commissioners and their personal staff who are political appointees and therefore subject to periodic change, the Commission's middle staff is comprised of career employees, many of whom have spent their entire working lives at the FCC. In addition, the middle staff exercises considerable influence because it controls the channels of communication to the commissioners. In choosing among various policy alternatives, the commissioners usually base their decisions on information provided by staff personnel. However, one former commissioner has complained that the FCC's decision-making process is dominated by entrenched bureau chiefs and agency coordinators who are reluctant to present alternatives to the commissioners for their consideration.[8]

Because hundreds of decisions must be made daily by the Commission, the formulation as well as the implementation of policy are frequently delegated to the Commission's middle staff. The result is a struggle for power within the FCC's hierarchy. Former Commissioner Nicholas Johnson believed too much authority was delegated to the middle staff:

Most matters are not handled at FCC meetings but are delegated by the Commission to the staff for action. In theory, these items are areas of settled Commission policy, but, in fact, the Commission has not so limited the scope of its delegations. During my term the majority has been unwilling to examine its delegation orders or to enunciate what standards control the delegation of decision-making authority.[9]

As with staff in any agency with active clientele groups, the FCC's staff is often tied to particular interests. Johnson provides an example:

The FCC's Cable Bureau is the cable industry's most vociferous advocate. Because a majority of the Commissioners are thought by the Cable Bureau to favor the broadcasting industry, it is apparently of the view that it must be an advocate for the other side. Compromise no doubt results from such an adversary process, but the best solution, in terms of the public interest, may not.[10]

Another former commissioner contends that a realistic understanding of bureaucratic decision making depends on a "recognition that the power motive is to bureaucracy what the profit motive is to business."[11] Government officials and staff generally maximize the influence of their positions, and the commissioners and staff of the FCC are no exception. Newly created bureaus and those hired to staff them justify and prolong their existence, even after their usefulness has ended.[12]

Another characteristic of bureaucracy that the Commission has exhibited relates to its concern for its own institutional survival. As a result, the FCC has a tendency to be inflexible, static, and conservative rather than adaptive, innovative, and creative. As a bureaucracy, the FCC is often reluctant to embrace innovative proposals, especially when such actions might mean the changing of familiar assumptions and standards.[13] Incremental change is favored over more comprehensive change. The Commission staff often feels it has little to gain by pushing for technological innovation and much to lose. Above all, the Commission favors process over substance, discussion over policymaking.

As with many other federal agencies, those below the level of political appointee at the FCC often resist changes promoted by the commissioners unless those changes are perceived as being consistent with the staff members' personal goals. The chairman of the Commission, for example, may find it difficult to persuade tenured staff members to take actions they consider inappropriate or illegitimate. A commissioner or chairman may have to spend many working days convincing the staff to follow his directives. However, commissioners may not be able or willing to devote such time to administrative tasks because they must perform time-consuming "public duties," such as meeting with industry representatives, public interest groups, members of the public, the press, and others. They may find working on internal administrative problems to be unrewarding and exhausting.

Therefore, a breakdown in administrative responsibility results. Although the Commission is an independent regulatory agency, it is very much a "political" body. It was created by Congress, which provides it with statutory authority and also exercises over it considerable oversight responsibility. Commissioners themselves are appointed by the President with the advice and consent of the Senate. Theoretically, the Commission learns from Congress and the executive branch what the "public interest" is in general terms and is "accountable" to those branches of government.

When staff members assume responsibilities and make policy decisions independent of directives from the top, the concept of responsibility breaks down. Congress holds the Commission "accountable" by oversight, budgeting, confirmation of appointees, and other methods. The courts hold the Commission "accountable" by judicial review, although they have problems monitoring Commission activities closely. When hierarchical functions become blurred, those overseeing Commission activity cannot easily trace responsibility for certain actions and decisions and hold those responsible accountable. Because the staff plays an increasingly important role in policymaking, the sources of important decisions are becoming increasingly hidden from public view.

Because regulatory commissions exercise "quasi-judicial" functions, it is particularly important that the reins of authority eventually converge into a relatively few pair of hands. Only with such convergence of authority will responsibility for actions be pinpointed.

The importance of administrative responsibility in a democratic system requires that administrative discretion be limited in any given situation to what is appropriate and necessary. Without such a check on administrative discretion, Congress, the public, and others will be unable to oversee the Commission.

As the staff of the Commission becomes increasingly specialized, the system of authority that results from a hierarchical system becomes less viable. The influential staff at the FCC tends to weaken the authority of those who would normally be held responsible. This situation may generate a great deal of conflict within the Commission itself. The commissioners sometimes find actions of the staff employees to be subversive.

In summary, when discussing the political environment of the FCC, a distinction must be made between the politically appointed commissioners, who may be at the Commission for a relatively short time, and career staff members, who, while less visible, exercise considerable influence over policymaking.

BACKGROUND OF COMMISSIONERS

The seven commissioners who sit at the top of the FCC's huge bureaucracy come from varied social and political backgrounds. The process by which they are selected is worth examining because it highlights much of the interaction and policy relationships among key actors in the FCC's environment.

Section 4(b) of the Communications Act of 1934 requires that no more than four of the seven commissioners be of the same political party. But a study of fifty-one appointments to the FCC and the FTC found that selections from the President's own party typically have been partisan choices, and the others have often been in sympathy with administration objectives rather than "bona fide, honest to God" members of the other party.[14]

The backgrounds of the forty-four individuals who served as FCC or Federal Radio Commission members between 1927 and 1961 have been analyzed in detail. Lawrence Lichty found that of the forty-four commissioners, twenty-three had studied law, twenty-four had some prior experience with broadcasting, and all but four had previously held government posts on either the federal or the state level. In short, the typical commissioner was trained in law, generally familiar with broadcasting, and quite likely to have had prior government administrative experience.[15]

An updated study analyzing the backgrounds of twenty-two commissioners who served between 1962 and 1975 found that the typical commissioner during this period had (1) some government affiliations; (2) strong political affiliations; and (3) some law experience.[16]

Perhaps the most important implication of such a common legal and administrative background is the FCC's tendency to see regulatory activities in legal and administrative terms rather than in social and economic terms.[17] Moreover, the backgrounds of the commissioners are more similar than is obvious: over the half century of appointments, only two blacks and three women have been appointed, with four of those five occurring in the 1970s.

INDIVIDUAL COMMISSIONERS

One should not assume, however, that the background characteristics of the commissioners enable one to predict how they will behave and what decisions they will make. Commissioners do exhibit factional behavior, and individual commissioners may play pivotal roles in decision making. Factions are, of course, not unique to the FCC. The individual dissenter, as with the courts, can be influential in later changing policy. As spokesman, the chairman can be particularly influential because of his larger staff and his greater visibility. He can significantly affect the planning of the Commission's work since he prepares the agenda for meetings and has a more direct relationship with bureau chiefs. In addition, the chairman can be instrumental in selecting and reappointing commissioners, especially if he has been helping the White House to further its goals. The study of FCC and FTC commissioners from 1949 to 1974 revealed that twelve of the fifty-one were selected largely because of the support of the Commission chairmen, and very few of those would have been nominated without such an endorsement.[18]

Individual commissioners have been successful in persuading the Commission to take certain positions, particularly if they hold the deciding vote. Some commissioners, such as Newton Minow, former chairman, and Nicholas Johnson, have worked outside the Commission to change the regulatory climate. Minow perceived a "hostile environment" partially paralyzing the Commission and decided "very early that of all the routes I might take to the best performance of my job, the most effective and the wisest road in the long run was to speak out in the hope of influencing public opinion about television . . . and so I went to the people with public speeches."[19] Minow was hoping that active public involvement in broadcasting would strengthen his position as chairman by creating public support for certain policies. In one speech, Minow shocked a convention of the National Association of Broadcasters when he characterized television as "a vast wasteland."[20] He challenged broadcasting executives to sit down in front of their television sets for a full day, assuring them they would observe a "vast wasteland" of game shows, violence, formula comedies, sadism, commercials, and boredom.[21]

Johnson attempted to promote greater participation by the public in broadcasting affairs and to encourage better public understanding of the role citizens should play in regulatory policymaking. In his book entitled *How to Talk Back to Your Television Set*,[22] Johnson alerted the public to its rights to challenge a broadcast licensee at renewal time. It was considered within the trade "the most unorthodox and unpopular thing an FCC commissioner had ever done."[23]

THE BROADCASTING INDUSTRY

Perhaps no actor or group of actors is more energetic in monitoring and attempting to influence FCC decisions than the broadcasters themselves. Barry Cole and Mal Oettinger vividly describe what happens to a commissioner after being appointed:

A Commission appointee realizes soon after coming to Washington that nobody ever heard of him or cares much what he does—except one group of very personable, reasonable, knowledgeable, delightful human beings who recognize his true worth. Obviously they might turn his head just a bit.[24]

The intricate and dynamic relationship between the FCC and interest/clientele groups plays a special role in shaping and interpreting FCC policies. Broadcasters are well organized and well financed and often seem a formidable influence at the Commission when compared to the underfunded public interest groups. On a day-to-day basis, FCC commissioners concern themselves with broadcasting problems, and naturally, they rely on the broadcasters for information and guidance. The problem, however, is that there is a thin line between gaining familiarity with an industry's problems and becoming biased in favor of that industry. As Johnson points out, the commissioners and their staff work closely with the industry and tend to see problems in industry terms:

If a person goes into industry, acquires friends in industry, goes to industry parties and conventions, sees his whole life-style determined by the vicissitudes of that industry, and acquires knowledge about the industry along the way, the paramount learning experience is not the subject matter but rather, the social framework in which it is acquired.[25]

The opinions and demands of the broadcasters are expressed through various groups and associations. As with any public organization, regulatory agencies must rely on groups for political support. Broadcasters provide much of that support through their lobbying organizations.

It would be inaccurate to assume that all broadcasters feel the same way on all issues. While sharing much in common, they are a heterogeneous group that may often find itself disagreeing on important issues. But there is clearly a sub-government comprised of congressional communications committees, the FCC, and the broadcasters that is the arena in which many policy decisions are made. The broadcasting "sub-government" includes the networks and multiple station owners, the Federal Communications Bar Association, *Broadcasting* magazine, the National Association of Broadcasters, the communication law firms, and the industry-hired public relations and management consultant firms. It also includes the permanent government staff—regulatory, executive and congressional—which is concerned with day-to-day activities of the broadcasting industry. People in this subgovernment typically spend their lives moving from one organization to another within it. Those who pursue the course of protecting the public interest are rarely admitted.[26]

The leading voice for the broadcasting industry is the National Association of Broadcasters, a trade organization with more than 4,900 member radio and television stations. The NAB has an annual budget of more than $5 million and a staff of over one hundred based in a $2.6 million building located only a few blocks from the FCC. Over the several decades that the NAB has been working on behalf of broadcasters, it has been remarkably successful in limiting efforts to place onerous regulatory burdens on broadcasting. The commercial time debate, to be discussed in the next chapter, is an example of its ability to rally broadcasters and to convince Congress not to place an additional requirement on broadcasters that would have limited the number of commercial minutes a radio or television station could broadcast.

In recent years, though, the NAB has had difficulty fending off congressional and FCC regulations of the broadcasting industry. In the last few decades, the climate in which broadcast regulation takes place has changed significantly. A number of reasons can be cited. The organizations represented by the NAB have grown in diversity and number so that other organizations have been created to lobby for special interests within the broadcasting industry.[27] The NAB cannot therefore present a united front on many regulatory policy issues, although it still is a force to be reckoned with.

Another reason for the change in regulatory climate is that the broadcasting industry no longer enjoys the same position that it did in the early decades of broadcast regulation when the process was dominated by Congress, the Commission, and the industry itself. In the last decade or so, other actors to be introduced include the public, in the form of citizen groups; the White House, by means of special advisory bodies and administrative offices; and as discussed in chapters 2 and 3, the courts, in the form of liberal rules of standing to allow a more "general" public interest and by judicial activism directed toward prescribing and precluding FCC policy initiatives. The development of these activist participants in broadcast regulation has modified the Commission's role and has forced the industry to share some of its influence and control over commission policy.

CITIZEN GROUPS

In recent years, citizen groups have attempted to establish administrative machinery for lobbying the Commission and Congress on broadcasting policy. While the organizations are small compared to the lobbying organizations of the broadcasters, they have been successful in forcing a broader definition of the public interest and have, on some occasions, forced the Commission to take certain actions. When the Commission and Congress are unwilling to respond to citizen demands, they have often chosen the courts as a vehicle for making policy. In the last ten years, such efforts have been very successful, although the Commission does not always fully comply.

The *WBLT* case discussed in chapter 3 allowed viewers and listeners to challenge FCC licensing decisions if they had an obvious and acute concern with licensing proceedings in order to make certain that broadcasters would be responsible to the needs of the audience. According to *Broadcasting* magazine, the *WLBT* case had consequences far beyond that specific case:

The case did more than establish the right of the public to participate in a station's license renewal hearing. It did even more than encourage minority groups around the country to assert themselves in broadcast matters at a time when unrest was growing and blacks were becoming more activist. It provided practical lessons in how pressure could be brought, in how the broadcast establishment could be challenged.[28]

While *Broadcasting* may exaggerate somewhat, the *WLBT* ruling did inspire groups to become active. The United Church of Christ, for example, the group that brought the *WLBT* case, is supported by various foundations and has helped hundreds of groups to monitor programming and to assess the employment practices of broadcast stations, even negotiating grievances with local broadcasters and preparing petitions to deny renewal applications.[29]

There are dozens of other media groups. Most recently, some primarily concerned with other matters began expressing displeasure over the amount of violence and sex on television. Often such groups have not simply directed their efforts toward the Commission but toward Congress as well. For example, Congress has been pressured by the Parent-Teachers Association and other groups to question the FCC about its television programming policies.

Senator John Pastore (D-Rhode Island), chairing the 1975 meeting of the Committee on Commerce, said, "We are interested in the Commission's actions in the critical area of children's television programming and any additional information with regard to its report to this committee concerning televised sex and violence in view of the action taken by broadcasters."[30] Congressional interest in television programming no doubt came from pressure from angry constituents urging Congress to improve television programming by limiting the amount of sex and violence.

The Commission has also attempted to make it easier for citizens to participate in its proceedings. Former FCC Chairman Richard Wiley, responding to a question about public participation from the chairman of the Senate Commerce Committee, Warren G. Magnuson (D-Washington), wrote that "participation by public groups in Commission proceedings is not a rarity. Such groups participate in hundreds of our proceedings annually. Increasingly, we find that they are well represented."[31]

The role of public interest groups in broadcasting policy was summed up by *Broadcasting*: "It is hard to find a community of any size without its organizations of blacks, Chicanos, Latinos, liberated women, activist mothers or other concerned types negotiating for stronger representation in broadcasting."[32]

THE WHITE HOUSE

Presidents have differed significantly in their interest in FCC activities. Some have demonstrated little interest beyond appointing commissioners; others have attempted to closely monitor FCC activities. For example, during the Kennedy, Johnson, and Nixon administrations, the FCC and other regulatory agencies sent detailed monthly summaries of their principal activities and pending projects to a key presidential aide. President Franklin D. Roosevelt had been very interested in FCC policy decisions, especially the question of ownership of radio stations by newspapers, but his successor, Harry Truman, showed little or no interest in commission policies. President Ford played a relatively passive role on issues concerning broadcasters.[33]

The Office of Management and Budget, part of the executive branch, is also important to the Commission. OMB reviews and revises all departmental and agency budget estimates before they are presented to the Appropriations committees of the House and the Senate. In addition, agencies such as the FCC must submit their legislative recommendations to OMB before asking for congressional consideration. OMB also has the power to authorize agencies to add "supergrade" staff positions. Some have expressed concern about the potential interference of OMB in Commission affairs and have suggested that the FCC's budget be submitted directly to Congress to further minimize OMB's influence.[34]

The National Telecommunications and Information Administration (NTIA), formerly the Office of Telecommunications Policy (OTP), has been involved with some issues traditionally left to the FCC. The function of the NTIA, located in the Commerce Department, is to advise the President on matters concerning communications policy. Much controversy has existed over whether the role of OTP and NTIA deprives the Commission of its ability to act in a "nonpartisan" manner, free from presidential interference. Under President Nixon, OTP Director Clay Whitehead did more than advise the President. The office developed complex rules regulating cable television, and Whitehead, in a speech delivered in 1973, was highly critical of the practices of the broadcast news media.[35] NTIA is interested in playing a more important role in shaping broadcasting policy and lobbying for such influence in the rewrite of the Communications Act.

The Justice Department, also an important actor in the FCC's political environment, represents the Commission in all legal matters except licensing. By selectively enforcing antitrust laws, the Justice Department can have a profound effect on communications matters. Its antitrust suits against the three major networks and its involvement in the FCC's cross-ownership rule-making proceedings gave the Justice Department formidable influence.[36]

CONGRESS

The FCC was created by Congress, is armed with statutory authority granted by Congress, and is funded by Congress. Perhaps it is understandable that many consider the Commission to be an ''arm'' of Congress.

When referring to congressional relations with the Commission, it is important to understand that Congress as a whole does not usually make regulatory policy. The vital groups in Congress relevant to broadcast regulation are the House and Senate Commerce committees, their respective communications subcommittees, and their chairmen. Other committees such as the Appropriations committees in each house demonstrate occasional interest in broadcasting issues, but clearly, the source of most activity is the communications subcommittees.

Congress has involved itself to a large degree in broadcasting policy, although it does not always demonstrate its interest through legislation. The Act that created the FCC has been largely unchanged for almost half a century, although it is currently being reexamined in Congress.

Even though the Commission was created as an independent regulatory agency, to Congress that means independence from

White House domination, not independence from Congress.

The power of Congress over the Commission is pervasive. The Commission enjoys relatively little protection from the President, although clientele groups do provide it with vital political support.

Congressional committees do not necessarily have to instruct the Commission in order to get favorable results. They simply need to create an atmosphere in which the "right" decisions are made:

> What matters here is not that an administrator is forced by a vote or an overt instruction of any legislative committee to initiate a particular policy, for seldom does this happen. More important is an administrator's assessment of the given ecology within which he must make his policy decisions. For efficacious policy initiation, he must attempt to perceive and anticipate the behavior of legislative committees and the environment reflected by them.[37]

Congressional interest and involvement in Commission activities can be traced somewhat to the importance of broadcasters to members' electoral success and public image. Congressmen who are sympathetic to the broadcasting industry may transmit their ideas and feelings to the Commission. Some have suggested that this is related to the financial interests some members of Congress hold in broadcasting properties. Until House and Senate financial disclosure statements were made public, it was impossible for the public to discover potential conflict of interests. These disclosure statements revealed that at least twenty-seven members of the House and thirteen Senators own outright or own stock in media worth at least $20 million.[38] Nine members of Congress own outright a newspaper, television station, or radio company; ten own controlling stock in forty-one newspapers and broadcast outlets; twenty-one own stock in major communications conglomerates.[39] Some even own media companies with outlets in their own districts.[40] But these data alone do not explain congressional interest in broadcasting issues. Such interest is more likely attributable to the facts that broadcasters are useful and important constituents and that voters sometimes express discontent over what they see on television.

Many members of Congress would rather not offend broadcasters. They exercise some control over the very lifeline of politicians—media exposure. An estimated 70 percent of the U.S. senators and 60 percent of the representatives regularly use free time offered by broadcasting stations back home.[41]

This is not to suggest that only members from safe districts are in positions to criticize broadcasters. But it is true that members concerned about reelection may hesitate to challenge the broadcasting industry if media outlets in their districts are controlled by broadcasting interests.

Congress oversees the FCC and influences regulatory policy in a number of ways. The most obvious is control by statute, although since 1934, Congress has passed relatively few laws affecting broadcasting. Control by statute is noteworthy for its relative unimportance. Congress was willing to grant in 1934 the broad mandate of regulating in the public interest, convenience, and necessity. The lack of substantive guidelines makes the Commission vulnerable to other forms of congressional influence. Importantly, because of the close relationship between Congress and the Commission, legislation has not been necessary to get the Commission to do what Congress wanted. A letter, a telephone call, a hearing, or a "raised eyebrow" is frequently enough.

The most important power that Congress exercises over the Commission is the power of the purse. Congress retains substantial discretion over the money allocated and the purposes for which the funds are to be used. Congressional authority resides primarily at the subcommittee level of the appropriations committees of both houses, which hold hearings each year to examine the FCC's budget requests and to question FCC commissioners and top staff. Many opportunities arise, both at the hearings and on other occasions, for committee members to scrutinize commission behavior and to communicate legislative desires to the officials involved.

The Commission also learns what Congress wants when committee reports are attached to appropriations bills. Although the reports are not law, the appropriations committees expect them to be regarded almost as seriously as if they were.[42] The congressional appropriations process makes it clear that the

FCC is not really an "independent" regulatory commission.

Few administrative or regulatory agencies have been subject to as much intense questioning during congressional hearings as the FCC. While some investigations have been hostile and critical and may even have damaged the Commission's reputation, others have called attention to problems at the Commission that were eventually corrected (for example, the "payola" scandals uncovered during the investigations in 1959-1960).

Finally, as mentioned before, individual congressmen can shape commission policy, for, as Minow pointed out, "it is easy—very easy—to confuse the voice of one congressman, or one congressional committee, with the voice of Congress."[43] Although the influence of individual members is hard to measure and rarely comes to public attention, these informal contacts may be more important than committee hearings.

The staff members of the relevant congressional committees maintain a close liaison with the FCC and often relay the views and expectations of their committee members to the commissioners and their staff. This relationship further enables Congress to maintain continual oversight of the Commission.

APPOINTMENT AND SERVICE OF COMMISSIONERS

Much can be learned about the FCC's political environment by examining the nature of the appointment process and the type of commissioners produced by the process.

Textbook descriptions of appointments to regulatory agencies say that the President, with the advice of his staff, nominates and that the Senate, after holding hearings, approves or disapproves the nominee. The reality, however, is much more complex and sheds light on the relationships between the White House and the FCC; the Congress and the FCC; the White House and the Congress; and all those actors' relationships with the broadcasters.

The process can be divided into four sections:[44] the identification and investigation; the nomination; the role of the Senate; and the departure of commissioners.

No more critical time in the appointment process exists than the identification and investigation phase, which precedes the actual decision to nominate. During this phase, the individuals who assist the President in dispensing patronage play a dominant role. Usually, the President is occupied with more important business, but every administration since Truman's has devised some system for identifying future vacancies and for recruiting and screening potential nominees.[45]

While some Presidents' staffs conduct organized searches for vacancies and for potential nominees to fill them, most appointees to the regulatory agencies are not picked as a result of a systematic search for talent. On the contrary, a majority of nominees are initially brought to the attention of the White House through either their own efforts or the efforts of their political sponsors. In other words, these positions are won after active campaigns are waged.

These campaigns are almost always conducted outside of public view. The public, relegated to secondary constituency status, is not included in perhaps the most crucial aspect of selecting FCC commissioners. While public attitudes may be considered when potential nominees are discussed, almost no effort is made to include participants from the general public.

The potential FCC nominee can be described as a "candidate." Often he appears to be waiting unknowingly on the side and agrees to a "draft," but most of the commissioners surveyed in the appointments study actively sought the job.

The appointments study suggested that campaigns for regulatory agencies may not always be successful but, as with elective office, may improve chances for future campaigns. The study stated that no less than seventeen of fifty-one persons appointed to the FCC and FTC between 1949 and 1974 received the appointment largely because of the carryover effect of a prior unsuccessful campaign. The study further stated:

Campaigns do not materialize out of thin air. They are carefully organized and diligently pursued. The candidate may be the moving force, or the opening efforts may be made by influential friends— in which case the candidate soon becomes actively involved. The campaigns that result from these efforts take no consistent form, even though they usually involve letters of recommendation, telephone calls, structuring of arguments on the candidate's behalf as well as identification of the competition.[46]

The regulated industries appear to have more of a veto in the selection process than a role in actively identifying future commissioners, although to specifically identify their role is difficult because much of the bargaining takes place informally. Broadcasters obviously follow the identification and selection process much more closely than do the general public and most members of Congress. Their interest in FCC appointments, no matter how diffused, is consistent and systematic. *Broadcasting* magazine, for example, probably monitors vacancies on the FCC more carefully than anyone, including those at the White House concerned with such matters.

The broadcasters are primarily concerned with the philosophy of the potential candidate. Is he pro- or anti-industry? The President does not have to appoint someone from industry to please the broadcasters. He needs only to appoint someone sympathetic and friendly to their interests.

Key congressmen offer the principal partisan political support for a candidate. Congressional interest in appointments is rooted in the notion that the commissions were created by Congress, vested with congressional authority, and are, therefore, arms of Congress. The extent of an individual member's influence on appointments will depend on how much power the congressman has in such areas and how much he is willing to expend to see a particular individual appointed. Naturally, the members of the communications committees are particularly interested in FCC appointments.

The President may or may not play an active role in the process that follows the nomination. Some Presidents do not even meet the nominee before the decision is made and the name sent to Congress. Some consider commission seats political "consolation" prizes and part of the presidential patronage system.

The selection process seems designed to reject "controversial" candidates. While there are exceptions, such as President Johnson's appointment of Nicholas Johnson to the FCC, controversial candidates are filtered out because the selection process is essentially a negative one. A potential nominee must overcome numerous obstacles, and actors in the FCC's environment exercise various degrees of veto power over the selection process. Key congressmen and industry figures may not always promote their candidate successfully, but they are likely to mount a well-organized campaign *against* a particular individual.

Selecting persons identified with the regulated industries has always been politically sensitive. While many believe that experience gained working in the industry provides helpful expertise, such overidentification with the industry makes it appear that the President is placing an insider in the important and sensitive position of regulating his own industry.

The public's attitude is usually considered only in a negative sense: ''Are they likely to object'' is how the question may be asked. Few appointees, for example, have been identified with consumer interests. From 1946 to 1975, only one appointee to either the FCC or FTC had nongovernment experience in consumer affairs.[47]

After the President makes the nomination, the Senate holds hearings and votes on confirmation. Based on the relatively litttle controversy that FCC nominees have encountered in the Senate, it is appropriate to conclude that much give-and-take bargaining takes place prior to the nomination. Of the fifty-one FCC and FTC commissioners appointed or reappointed during the period covered in the appointments study, there were not more than a dozen instances of controversy in the Senate, and only on four occasions did the nomination reach the point of a rollcall vote. From 1953 to 1972, no FCC or FTC nominee was rejected on the floor of the Senate, and only two were withdrawn by the President before the Senate acted.

Not all Senate hearings, however, have been routine. On September 21, 1973, only three months after the Senate rejected his nominee to the Federal Power Commission, President Nixon nominated a former broadcaster, James Quello, as an FCC commissioner. Because of objections from various consumer groups and congressmen, the Senate held an eight-day hearing on the Quello nomination (the longest hearing ever conducted for an FCC nominee) and delayed confirmation for seven months. Eventually, the Senate confirmed Quello, but Chairman of the Senate Commerce Committee, Magnuson, expressed concern over the quality of Nixon's regulatory appointments:

We have always given the President—without regard to party—the benefit of the doubt on [regulatory] appointments—But I must tell you that we have swallowed nominees by [the Nixon] administration who have left a bitter aftertaste, and our tolerance for mediocrity and lack of independence from economic interests is rapidly coming to an end.[48]

Despite these problems, relatively few nominees have faced substantial opposition. It is safe to conclude, therefore, that much of the confirmation process occurs away from public view, during the identification and decision to nominate stage.

The final phase in the entire process is the departure of commissioners and their subsequent careers. Although many reasons may come into play, significantly just over one-third of the FCC commissioners complete a full term, and chairmen are even less likely to complete a full seven-year term.

The reasons why so few commissioners complete a full term have been the subject of much discussion. One reason could be termed psychological; after a period of time, the challenge inherent in the position may diminish, attraction fades, and the commissioner begins to consider other possibilities. Income is also a factor. Many commissioners could earn much higher salaries in the broadcasting or in other industries than they do on the Commission. The concern over reappointment is another factor. Holdovers from previous administrations can never be certain of reappointment.

Although it has never been done, Congress has the authority to remove a commissioner by impeachment. The President's power is far less clear, and the Communications Act of 1934 is silent on the issue. The Supreme Court has indicated that a President cannot remove a sitting commissioner simply because he wants to appoint someone of his own choosing. Nor is disagreement over policy sufficient cause for removing a member of the regulatory agencies.[49]

On the issue of subsequent careers, there is the widely held notion that, because of the contacts they have made and the expertise they have acquired, the regulatory commissioners "cash in" handsomely after their agency service. The appointments study concluded, however, that, although the prospects for some have been financially brighter after leaving their commission posts, these jobs rarely lead to higher office, whether appointive or elective. The vast majority do remain in Washington and eventually do serve the interests they once regulated. Of thirty-one FCC commissioners who served between 1952 and 1975, fourteen became privately employed in agency-related work.

CONCLUSION

This chapter has examined the political environment in which the Federal Communications Commission regulates the broadcasting industry. It was indicated that actors in the environment exercise varying degrees of influence over FCC policy making and that a group of "primary" actors are particularly active in broadcasting issues.

Concluding a detailed article on one day in the life of the FCC, Johnson suggested that the courts may be the best vehicle by which to protect the public's interest in broadcasting:

A final purpose of this article, then, is to offer the judicial branch some idea of how bad things really are, of how tenuous is the basis for the idea that judges should defer to the FCC's "rational and orderly" process. Long-range reforms aside, if there is to be any immediate hope for the FCC, it lies with the courts.[50]

The next chapter will consider a number of specific policies and the interaction among the various actors in shaping those policies. It will argue, moreover, that the public interest does not necessarily emerge out of the clashing of these various interests.

NOTES

1. Erwin G. Krasnow and Lawrence D. Longley, *The Politics of Broadcast Regulation* (New York: St. Martin's Press, 1978), p. 7.

2. Normally, the trade press would not be considered an actor in an agency's environment but would simply serve to convey information about the industry and government regulation of that industry. In the case of the FCC's regulation of broadcasting, there is a virtual trade press monopoly, and one magazine, *Broadcasting*, plays a significant role in shaping communications policy.

3. See particularly Anthony Downs, *Inside Bureaucracy* (Boston: Little, Brown and Company, 1967).

4. United States Senate, Committee on Commerce, 94th Congress, 2d Session, "Appointments to the Regulatory Agencies: The Federal Communications Commission and the Federal Trade Commission, 1949-1974)," April 1976. Hereafter, this document will be referred to as the appointments study.

5. Walter B. Emery, *Broadcasting and Government: Responsibilities and Regulation* (East Lansing: Michigan State University Press, 1971), p. 57.

6. Obviously, the extent to which each commissioner influenced policy decisions depended on numerous factors.

7. 66 Stat. 712-713.

8. Krasnow and Longley, p. 29.

9. Nicholas Johnson and John Jay Dystel, "A Day in the Life: The Federal Communications Commission," 82 *Yale Law Journal* (July 1973): 1576.

10. Ibid., p. 1596.

11. Krasnow and Longley, p. 29.

12. Ibid.

13. Ibid., p. 30.

14. Appointments study, pp. 385-86.

15. Lawrence Lichty, "Members of the Federal Radio Commission and Federal Communications Commission: 1927-1961," 6 *Journal of Broadcasting* (Winter 1961-1962): 23-34.

16. Wenmouth Williams, Jr., "Impact of Commissioner Background on FCC Decisions: 1962-1975," 20 *Journal of Broadcasting* (Spring 1976): 239-44.

17. Krasnow and Longley, p. 32.

18. Appointments study, pp. 185-95.

19. Newton Minow, *Equal Time: The Private Broadcaster and the Public Interest* (New York: Atheneum, 1964), pp. ix-x.

20. Krasnow and Longley, p. 37.

21. "Minow Observes a 'Vast Wasteland,' " *Broadcasting* (May 15, 1960): 58-59.

22. Nicholas Johnson, *How to Talk Back to Your Television Set* (Boston: Little, Brown and Company, 1967).

23. Les Brown, *Television: The Business Behind the Box* (New York: Harcourt Brace Jovanovich, 1971), pp. 256-57.

24. Barry Cole and Mal Oettinger, "Covering the Politics of Broadcasting," *Columbia Journalism Review* (November/December 1977): 58.

25. Appointments study, p. 398.

26. Nicholas Johnson, "A New Fidelity to the Regulatory Ideal," 59 *Georgetown Law Journal* (March 1971): 884.

27. Groups now protect the interests of television stations (Association of Maximum Service Telecasters); television translator stations (National Translator Association); UHF television stations (Council for UHF Broadcasting); clear channel AM radio stations (Clear Channel Broadcasting Service); daytime AM radio stations (Daytime Broadcasters Association); stations owned by blacks (National Association of Black-Owned Stations); religious stations (National Religious Broadcasters); and AM and FM stations (National Radio Broadcasters Association). Krasnow and Longley, p. 42.

28. "The Pool of Experts on Access," *Broadcasting Magazine* (September 20, 1971): 36.

29. Krasnow and Longley, p. 45.

30. Committee on Commerce, United States Senate, "Oversight of the Federal Communications Commission," April 21 and 22, 1975, p. 1.

31. United States Senate, Commerce Committee, "Agency Comments on the Payment of Reasonable Fees for Public Participation in Agency Proceedings," January 1977, p. 11. Wiley's letter was written December 22, 1976.

32. Leonard Zeidenberg, "The Struggle Over Broadcast Access II," *Broadcasting Magazine* (September 27, 1971): 24.

33. Krasnow and Longley, p. 56.

34. Robert E. Lee, "The FCC and Regulatory Duplication: A Case of Overkill?" 51 *Notre Dame Lawyer* (December 1975): 246.

35. Clay T. Whitehead, "Broadcasters and the Network: The Responsibility of the Local Station," 39 *Vital Speeches* (February 1, 1973): 230.

36. Paul Laskin, "Shadowboxing with the Networks," *The Nation* (June 14, 1975):715.

37. William W. Boyer, *Bureaucracy on Trial: Policy Making by Government Agencies* (Indianapolis/Bobbs-Merrill, 1964), p. 42.

38. Tracy Freedman, "Strange Bedfellows: Congressmen Who Own Media," *Washington Journalism Review* (September/October 1978): 58.

39. Ibid.

40. Ibid., p. 59.

41. Robert MacNeil, *The People Machine: The Influence of Television on American Politics* (New York: Harper & Row, 1968), p. 246.

42. Krasnow and Longley, p. 74.

43. Minow, p. 35.

44. Appointments study, p. 375.

45. Ibid., p. 376.

46. Ibid., p. 378.

47. That unusual event occurred in 1949, when President Truman appointed John Carson to the FTC.

48. Krasnow and Longley, p. 84.

49. *Humphrey's Executor v. United States*, 295 U.S. 602 (1935); and *Wiener v. United States*, 357 U.S. 349 (1958).

50. Johnson and Dystel, p. 1634.

5.
Broadcasting and the Public Interest: Access and Diversity

Broadcasting companies are not in business to serve First Amendment principles. They are profit making businesses that exhibit many of the same characteristics of any other enterprise whose goal is to maximize profits. Yet these firms market an unusually important commodity, communication, and are therefore subject to standards different from those applied to other industries.

Since federal regulation began some fifty years ago, the broadcasting industry has become one of the most powerful and important in the country. Its success can be measured, in part, by its financial success. In 1979, the last year for which official FCC figures are available, commercial broadcasting had total revenues of 10.6 billion and profits of 1.9 billion. Television accounted for 7.9 billion (74.5 percent) and 1.7 billion (89.5 percent) of profits. Radio accounted for 2.7 billion (25.5 percent) in revenues and 241 million (10.5 percent) of profits. Public broadcasting had a 1979 income of 603.5 million, of which 27 percent came from the federal government.[1]

In short, the broadcasting business can be very profitable, and the license granted by the federal government to broadcasters can be quite valuable.

When the Commission chooses among applicants for a license, it not only "silences" those rejected, it deprives them of potentially huge revenues. Congress, which is "rewriting" the Communications Act of 1934, is considering charging a user-fee based on the value of the license.[2]

During the last half century, broadcasters have vociferously fought increased government regulation, particularly when it affects the revenue-generating segments of the industry. However, they remain ambivalent toward policy that infringes on their First Amendment rights.

LIMITING COMMERCIAL TIME

On March 28, 1963, the Federal Communications Commission announced that it was considering policies designed to control the number and frequency of advertisements broadcast by radio and television stations. Although long concerned about advertising abuses, the FCC had not proposed formal rules until 1963. The Commission recognized the broadcasters' efforts to regulate themselves, but it found "abundant evidence" that the codes of the National Association of Broadcasters, which among other things limited the time that can be devoted to commercials, were being ignored by some stations and networks.[3]

The broadcasters mounted a campaign in Congress to prevent the Commission from setting advertising limits. The House considered a bill denying the Commission power to set such limits throughout 1963 and into early 1964. On February 24, 1964, the National Association of Broadcasters dispatched memos to all broadcast stations marked:

"Urgent Urgent Urgent": Broadcasters should immediately urge their Congressmen by phone or wire to vote for H.R. 8316. . . . A vote for the bill is a vote of confidence in the broadcasters in his district. A vote against the bill would open the door to unlimited governmental control of broadcasting.[4]

Three days later, the House passed the bill by a vote of 317 to 43. While the Senate never took action, the composition of the FCC changed shortly after the House vote, and by a majority of 4-3, the Commission rescinded its intention to set such rules, warning that extreme cases would still be considered at license renewal time.

Broadcasters have not, however, been so diligent or enthusiastic in pressing First Amendment claims, as for example, by appealing U.S. Court of Appeals decisions mandating increased attention to fairness doctrine responsibilities. Although such content regulation as the fairness doctrine, personal attack, and equal time rules do not go uncriticized or unnoticed by broadcasters, they do show less commitment to First Amendment ideals than to protesting policies that affect commercial interests.

UHF TELEVISION

Broadcasters have demonstrated much interest in preventing potential competitors from gaining access to the airwaves. During the 1950s, the FCC had the opportunity to make UHF (Ultra High Frequency) television a viable entity. The advantage of UHF, as opposed to VHF (Very High Frequency), is the increased number of channels available in the UHF band. Only twelve channels are available on the VHF band, but more than fifty are on the UHF band (Some technical problems, however, are associated with broadcasting on the higher frequencies).

In 1952, the Commission issued its Sixth Report and Order, on television allocations, which rejected "all-UHF" television—either nationally or in selected areas—as economically disastrous for existing broadcasting. As a result, UHF faced crippling competition from established, economically secure VHF stations.[5]

For some time, the Commission seriously considered "deintermixture" of seven markets then assigned both VHF and UHF stations. The Commission, if it had followed through, would have made those seven markets all UHF, the theory being that if UHF stations did not compete with VHF stations they would prosper financially. Established broadcasting interests objected strenuously and convinced the Commission that uprooting existing VHF stations would be too politically costly. Moreover, a strong possibility existed that Congress, under pressure from VHF broadcasters, would have denied the Commission the power to implement such a plan.

Eventually, a compromise was worked out. After several years' debate, Congress passed the All-Channel Receiver Law granting the Commission rule-making authority to provide that all television sets shipped in interstate commerce be equipped to receive both VHF and UHF television. The Commission adopted this rule, which went into effect April 30, 1964.

The threat of "deintermixture" was the major reason that the All-Channel Receiver Law was passed. Clearly, broadcasters were willing to expend considerable resources and energy to fight proposals that they viewed as threatening to their economic interests. While the concept of diversity lies at the core of the First Amendment, broadcasters were not much interested in diversity, for it is tantamount to increased competition. Public television, with its relatively small audiences, is probably the exception; commercial broadcasters appear to welcome its existence.

FM BROADCASTING

The way the Commission treated FM broadcasting in the 1940s further illustrates the broadcasters' ability to squelch competition. FM broadcasting actually developed in the 1930s and, because of a number of characteristics, had advantages over AM broadcasting, including (1) a static-free signal; (2) increased frequency range allowing for high-fidelity broadcasting; (3) the ability for one FM station to exist quite close to other FM stations on the same frequency without the mutual interference experienced with AM; (4) the opportunity for a significant increase in broadcast competition through large numbers of new stations in a new frequency band; and (5) the challenge to network control of programming through diversification of broadcasting services.[6]

These advantages made FM a potential threat to the dominance of existing AM broadcasting. After years of debate, the Commission eventually decided to move all FM broadcasting to a substantially higher band, thus making room for television, which emerged during the final years of World War II. Many of the large broadcasting companies that were successfully operating AM radio stations were anxious to enter television. The turf occupied by FM, because of the technical advantages, became most appealing.

Despite the fact that all FM receivers were made inoperative, the Commission on June 27, 1945, shifted the entire FM band. The Commission claimed that the move was made because the space previously occupied by FM was subject to interference by sunspots and other technical problems. This argument is questionable, however, considering the subsequent assignment of the same frequencies to television, which is far more susceptible to interference than is FM, and later to land mobile services such as police and fire department radios, where static-free service is even more crucial.[7]

The growth and eventual emergence of FM broadcasting were set back until the late 1950s and early 1960s, when the high-fidelity boom and the development of FM stereo enabled it to achieve the status expected of it fifteen years earlier.

COMPARATIVE RENEWAL

The comparative renewal policies of the Commission are of vital interest to the broadcasters. Few areas of broadcasting policy have been as turbulent in recent years as the rules governing the conditions under which an incumbent broadcaster's license is taken away and awarded to someone else.

The FCC conducts licensing hearings in three types of situations:

1. When determining whether or not to renew the license of an existing television or radio station, even though that license is not being sought by other parties. (Such hearings are rare since most licenses are renewed without a hearing.)

2. When several applicants compete for a *new* broadcast station.

3. When applicants compete for an *existing* station. (This is the most controversial area.)

For the most part, broadcasters have been successful in making it extremely difficult and rare for a challenger to take away a license from an incumbent broadcaster. Moreover, the Commission has been very hesitant not to renew a license, even when a broadcaster's record has been unusually poor. As discussed in chapter 3, the Commission even refused to take away the license of WLBT-TV in Jackson, Mississippi, despite its segregationist record. Only after the U.S. Court of Appeals for the District of Columbia ordered the license taken away did the Commission reluctantly comply.[8]

However, the Commission did refuse to renew the license of WHDH-TV in Boston (also discussed in chapter 3), an action that sparked much fear in the broadcasting industry. For the first time, the Commission refused to renew the license of a station that had an "average" record of performance, awarding it instead to an applicant that promised to be more active in the station's operation and to add to the diversity of control over mass communications media in the Boston area.[9] (The decision not to renew WHDH's license was also based on other grounds such as illegal *ex parte* contacts between WHDH and the chairman of the Federal Communications Commission.)

In the wake of the WHDH decision, broadcasters exerted pressure on congressmen and a number of bills were introduced dealing with the comparative renewal process. Senate Bill 2004, introduced by Senator John Pastore (D-Rhode Island), would have amended section 309 of the Communications Act to provide that the Commission could not consider competing applications for a license at renewal time unless it had first found, based on the licensee's renewal application, "that a grant of the application of a renewal applicant would not be in the public interest, convenience and necessity."[10] The Supreme Court, in *Ashbacker Radio Corporation v. F.C.C.*,[11] had interpreted section 309 to mean that when two or more applicants are mutually exclusive the Commission must conduct one full comparative hearing.[12] While *Ashbacker* involved two original applications, "no one has seriously suggested that its principle does not apply to renewal proceedings as well."[13]

Despite the apparent unconstitutionality of S. 2004, it appeared headed for quick passage. Hearings on the bill were held by the Senate Communications Subcommittee on August 5, 6, and 7, 1969, during which all but one of the witnesses testified in favor of the bill. A combination of events, however, impeded the momentum, and some congressmen became concerned that passage of S. 2004 would give a broadcaster a license in perpetuity.[14]

When a number of interest groups, including Black Efforts for Soul in Television (BEST) and the Citizens Communications Center (CCC), protested, some members of Congress, including some sponsors of the bill, began to have second thoughts. BEST picketed NAB offices in Washington, New York, and Los Angeles and network-owned stations in Boston, Chicago, Philadelphia, and San Francisco. The picketers read the following statement:

This bill represents backdoor racism because it is a subtle, and therefore more vicious, attempt to limit the efforts of the black community to challenge the prevailing racist practices of the vast majority of TV stations. . . . The Pastore Bill attempts to keep the media safely in the grips of monopolistic and politically selfish private white owners. It would deny black citizens the opportunity to demonstrate their ability to manage a TV station in a manner more consistent with the public interest than the station's present white owners. . . . Senator Pastore seeks to protect the media barons who operate to satisfy their personal economic greed.[15]

Eventually, Congress lost interest in S. 2004, and it was never passed. However, the Commission all but adopted it on January 15, 1970, when it issued its Policy Statement on Comparative Hearings Involving Regular Renewal Applicants. Under the policy statement, the renewal hearing was divided into two stages. In the first stage, the past performance of the applicant for renewal would be examined. If the renewal applicant showed "that its program service during the preceding license term has been substantially attuned to meeting the needs and interests of its area and that the operation of the station has not otherwise been characterized by serious deficiencies . . . his application for renewal will be granted."[16] If the examiner found that the applicant's service had not been so attuned, the hearing would continue into the second stage during which the incumbent licensee would be deprived of any preference due to incumbency. The Commission defended favoring an incumbent as necessary to preserve industry stability.

Commissioner Nicholas Johnson, providing the one dissenting vote to the FCC's action, believed that:

> The impact of citizen outrage measurably slowed the progress of S. 2004, and many Senate observers began to predict the Bill would never pass. Then, without formal rule making hearings, or even submission of written arguments, the Commission suddenly issues its January 15, 1970 Policy Statement—achieving much of what Congress had been unable or reluctant to adopt.
>
> There were many parties who had invested substantial time and money fighting the threatened dimunition of their rights. . . . By refusing even to listen to their counsels, this Commission has reached a new low in its self-imposed isolation from the people; once again we closed our ears and minds to their pleas.[17]

On April 1, 1970, CCC and BEST challenged the legality of the policy statement in the U.S. Court of Appeals for the District of Columbia. During the summer of 1970, while the case was pending, the staff of the Special Subcommittee on Investigations of the House Committee on Interstate and Foreign Commerce, looked into the Commission's policy statement. In a report issued in November 1970, the staff charged that the policy statement "is not a policy but a flagrant attempt to repeal the statutory requirements and to substitute the FCC's own legislative proposal that a hearing is not required when it involves a license renewal proceeding having several competing applicants."[18] The study further claimed that

> [it] was not until now that any agency has had the temerity to usurp congressional power and by way of a "policy statement" repeal a constitutional and statutory requirement in the interest of easing Commission workload requirements.
>
> [The policy statement] exemplifies both an unwarranted solicitude for the economic well-being of the licensee who enjoys a wealth-producing permit to use the public's precious airwaves and an indifference to the public interest including the rights of viewers and listeners to have access to viewpoints and programs from diversified sources.[19]

On June 11, 1971, a three-judge panel of the Court of Appeals struck down the policy statement and ordered that the Commission redesignate all comparative renewal hearings to reflect the court's judgment. Judge J. Skelly Wright, writing for a unanimous court, held:

By depriving competing applicants of their right to a full comparative hearing on the merits of their own applications, and by severely limiting the importance of other comparative criteria, the Commission has made the cost of processing a competing application prohibitive when measured by the challengers' very minimal chances of success.[20]

The Communications Act is silent on the issue of preferring an incumbent at license renewal time. Nevertheless, Commission policy has promoted stability in the broadcasting industry, which must have given special advantages to the incumbent. The court felt, however, that Commission policies had evolved to "give an incumbent a virtually insuperable advantage on the basis of his past record of past programming performance."[21] Coupled with the unavoidable uncertainty over the challenger's ability to carry out its program proposals, Commission policy made it extremely difficult to abrogate a license.

The court was very critical of what it viewed as a Commission effort to enact the provisions of S. 2004, which even Congress had failed to approve. Only upon refusal to renew because of the incumbent's past failure to provide substantial service would full comparative hearings be held. To the court, the Commission's action "administratively" enacted what the Pastore bill sought to do. The court held that this violated Section 309's requirements of a full hearing. Judge Wright considered the suggestion that the Commission can do without notice and hearing in a policy statement what Congress failed to do is, to say the least, "remarkable."

The comparative renewal case clearly demonstrates the broadcasters' concern about competition. They successfully convinced the Commission to take action even when Congress had failed to do so. The Commission must have understood the political risks involved. While the congressional staff report discussed above was never acted upon, it did provide some indication of congressional response to the Commission's policy statement. The scolding by the U.S. Court of Appeals also indicated the unpopularity of the Commission's decisions with nonbroadcasters. Nevertheless, the Commission was persuaded by broadcasters concerned about their economic interests to draw up and issue the policy statement.

The question becomes, then, the extent to which broadcasters promote and protect their First Amendment privileges and responsibilities, as opposed to their economic interests. A related issue concerns whether broadcasters should be punished if they fail to live up to those First Amendment responsibilities. Tucked away in Judge Wright's opinion are words that shed light on that issue:

> The suggestion that the possibility of nonrenewal, however remote, might chill uninhibited, robust and wide-open speech cannot be taken lightly. But the Commission, of course, may not penalize exercise of First Amendment rights. And the statute does provide for judicial review. Indeed, the failure to promote the full exercise of First Amendment freedoms through the broadcast medium may be a consideration against license renewal. Unlike totalitarian regimes, in a free country there can be no authorized voice of government. Though dependent on government for its license, independence is perhaps the most important asset of the renewal applicant.[22]

This is a remarkable statement. If, in fact, broadcasters' ambivalence toward First Amendment principles has made them less than diligent in pressing for First Amendment freedoms, then such an attitude can be considered when the licensee is evaluated at renewal time. If, as has been suggested, broadcasters have demonstrated much greater interest in protecting their revenue-generating activities from government regulation than in protecting the First Amendment, then such lack of allegiance to First Amendment principles hardly entitles them to be free from the fairness doctrine, personal attack rules, and other rules designed to promote diversity and access. While broadcasters' claims that these rules dilute the vitality of the First Amendment have some merit, greater attention to public affairs and controversial issues would not automatically follow if the rules are repealed. In the absence of greater commitment to public affairs programming, Congress will probably not agree that the First Amendment should apply to electronic media as fully as it does to the print media.

Ideally, diversity is achieved by market forces and with a minimum of government interference. It should be a matter of great concern that the medium by which most people now claim they get their news—television—is so heavily regulated by the federal government. But in a monopoly environment that exists despite current technologies, and where entrance is limited by the availability of scarce frequencies, market forces are not sufficiently strong to ensure diversity. In fact, under the current regulatory system, there is a remarkable lack of diversity.[23] As the chairman of the Federal Communications Commission recently noted:

> The real problem we face concerning networks today is not that they exist, but that there are so few of them. There is no magic in the number "3". Economics may dictate that stations in different markets will cooperate in some organizational form to select programs, gather news and sell advertising time. But it is not clear that there is room for only three networks. Nor is it clear that any new networks, to survive in the national market, must be of equal size and strength to those that now exist.[24]

Some indications exist that there is the potential for much greater diversity without intolerable levels of government interference. Still, government-imposed standards of fairness and diversity do affect substantial First Amendment interests and cannot be taken lightly.

Theoretically, increased competition and access could minimize the government's role in determining the content of news and entertainment programming. Such rules as the fairness doctrine do affect content. But the broadcasters who have successfully fought potential competition have "settled" for government regulation that affects First Amendment interests but that does not limit revenues. The fairness doctrine requires that controversial issues of public importance be presented fairly. When the Commission decides that a program or set of programs do not include the required balance, it seeks to provide access for those who would otherwise not have their views discussed. This type of diversity costs the broadcasters significantly less than diversity arising from increased competition. Broadcasters have, therefore, favored "fairness doctrine diversity" over "competition diversity" because of the former's minor impact on revenue-generating activities.

Broadcasters' uncertain commitment to establishing their full First Amendment rights does not mean that they are universally disinterested. NBC's expensive defense in the *Pensions* case is an example of the commitment sometimes demonstrated in defense of the First Amendment.[25] Within broadcasting companies, news and other departments concerned with public affairs have often vehemently protested Commission and court incursions into First Amendment areas. But that commitment has not been translated into fulfilling the Part One requirement of the fairness doctrine. Few documentaries are shown during prime time, and locally produced public affairs programming is generally uninformative and sometimes unwatchable. Local access periods, mandated by the Commission's "prime-time" access rules, have often been used not for local or even for nationally produced public affairs programming but for syndicated situation comedies, game shows, and the like.[26] Many stations broadcast very little or no local public affairs programming. The National Citizens Committee for Broadcasting (NCCB) has proposed that each television station be required to provide at least "one hour per week of regularly scheduled, prime time, *locally-originated* public affairs programming."[27] NCCB's proposal is worthy of careful consideration.

Broadcasters have argued that self-regulation achieves diversity best because it damages the First Amendment least. While this argument has theoretical merit, broadcasters cannot use their past performance to show how self-regulation creates an environment in which a multitude of voices discuss issues of public importance.

The First Amendment must be flexible enough to protect forms of speech that could not be contemplated by the Framers. Applying eighteenth-century principles to twentieth-century broadcasting has been difficult. But at the core of the First

Amendment, whether the context is the eighteenth, or the twentieth century, is the concept of diversity. Nowhere is the role of the First Amendment in promoting diversity discussed with more eloquence than in Justice William Brennan's majority opinion in *New York Times v. Sullivan*:[28]

Thus we consider this case against the background of a profound national commitment to the principle that debate on public issues should be uninhibited, robust, and wide-open, and that it may well include vehement, caustic, and sometimes unpleasantly harsh attacks on government and public officials.[29]

Justice Brennan believed, as did Justice Holmes before him, that a democratic system relies on the availability of information and on the uninhibited exchange of ideas. Our constitutional history is rich with those who felt our very freedom depended on the ability of citizens to learn about their government and to make intelligent decisions as voters. While the First Amendment does not contain the word "diversity," clearly it lies at its core.

Related to, but separate from, diversity is the question of responsibility. The First Amendment grants special status to the press, thus charging it with responsibilities that apply to no other institutions. Newspaper journalism, so deeply ingrained in our political minds, is largely immune from government-imposed standards of responsibility and fairness. No newspaper in the United States has a constitutional duty to serve in the public interest. If a partisan newspaper refuses to cover the activities of the opposition party, no federal or state government can do anything about it.

In broadcasting, however, concern exists for those "silenced voices" deprived access because they were unable to secure a license. Thus, complex rules provide those voices the opportunity to express their sentiments before the public. To many, such rules as the fairness doctrine and personal attack rules do not provide access for those voices and do harm to the First Amendment rights of broadcasters. Some argue that a "hands-off" approach not only would promote diversity and responsibility but also would prevent further erosion of the First Amendment. This argument, moreover, is based on a remarkable lack of diversity in television programming: during the half-century of federal regulation, twenty-five of which included television, broadcasting has shown relatively little diversity. Regulation of broadcasting cripples the First Amendment, it is argued, and creates censorship. Such critics of regulation argue that the fairness doctrine has not fostered debate on controversial issues of public importance but has resulted in bland programming and in a minimal effort to provide a forum to discuss public issues.[30]

In addition, the "impact rationale" has led some to maintain that, since broadcasting is now so pervasive, government must actively protect individuals from its harmful effects. Justice John Paul Stevens, writing the majority opinion in *Federal Communications Commission v. Pacifica Foundation*, said:

> The broadcast media have established a uniquely pervasive presence in the lives of all Americans. Patently offensive, indecent material presented over the airwaves confronts the citizen, not only in public, but also in the privacy of the home, where the individual's right to be let alone plainly outweighs the First Amendment rights of the intruder.[31]

It is difficult to square such "impact rationality" with historically conceived First Amendment principles. A newspaper has a large circulation and may be pervasive in its locale, but government regulation is still not warranted. Although it must be remembered that Justice Stevens is discussing "indecent" material, he does suggest that the pervasiveness of American broadcasting provides greater constitutional justification for governmental regulation, even though pervasiveness or lack of competition has never justified regulating newspapers. When ruling on the constitutionality of a law that was designed to increase diversity and access and to protect individual rights in print media, a unanimous Supreme Court in *Miami Herald v. Tornillo* held that it "failed to clear the barriers of the First Amendment."[32]

The government's "hands-off" policy toward print media has provided two centuries of experience to guide the regulation of the much younger broadcasting industry.[33] Yet even in the print media, market forces have largely failed to promote diversity, as indicated in the discussion in chapter 1. Should market forces be allowed to work in the broadcasting field? The question is of particular significance considering that the technical capability now exists to greatly increase the number of radio and television stations. Unfortunately, today few of these new stations could be operated at a profit. Still, satellite communications and cable television provide the potential for many more stations than are currently on the air. The established broadcasting interests have been relatively successful in getting the Commission to impede the development of the new technologies through regulation. Cable television, broadcasting's fierce competitor, had largely been "regulated to death," although the U.S. Court of Appeals for the District of Columbia refused to allow the Commission to strangle the industry completely.[34]

In addition to new technology, public television provides the potential for increased diversity. While public television has had funding problems, and is vulnerable to harassment by determined members of the executive branch (as during the Nixon administration), it may still provide the most immediate source of divergent programming. The "rewrite" of the Communications Act, if enacted in its present form, would provide that commercial broadcasters be charged user fees for their frequency and that part of the money raised would supplement the budget of public broadcasting.[35] Although some are concerned about the user fee itself and about forcing public broadcasting to rely on it, public television would be much better funded than it has been.[36]

Finally, the First Amendment, while not providing enforcement mechanisms, commands broadcasters as well as their print counterparts to provide the public with information to make intelligent decisions and to be informed on public issues. Broadcasting is different from newspapers in this regard because it is not predominantly in the business of providing news. The majority of broadcast time is devoted to entertainment, not to public affairs. Chapter 1 suggested that there exists not only a First Amendment right to broadcast but also a First Amendment right to be informed on issues of public importance.

Coverage of such issues varies greatly. In the *Columbia Journalism Review*, Ron Powers surveyed the amount of time local stations devoted to news and public affairs. The ten stations devoting the largest percentage of the broadcast day to news and public affairs ranged from 16.7 to 13.3 percent.[37] The ten stations showing the least amount of news and public affairs programming ranged from 4.1 to 5.9 percent. The botton ten included television stations located in such cities as Minneapolis (the fourteenth largest television market in the country),[38] Indianapolis (twentieth market),[39] Kansas City (twenty-seventh market),[40] and Nashville (thirty-first market).[41] All of the stations are network affiliates and are located in markets large enough to provide the owners with substantial revenues. The stations that devoted from 4.1 to 5.9 percent of their programming to news and public affairs obviously did not consider their primary responsibility to be disseminating such information.

Part of this lack of commitment to news and public affairs programming lies with the Commission, which, although it does require licensees to report on their news and public affairs programming, has no minimum time that must be devoted to such to ensure the granting or renewal of a license. The Commission has delegated to its staff the authority to renew automatically the licenses of network-affiliated television stations that have proposed more than 5 percent "informational (news plus public affairs)" programming, assuming the renewal is otherwise uncontested and proper.[42] If a licensee has included less than 5 percent in its broadcast schedule, the renewal must be referred to the full Commission for review. Remarkably, then, a major station is considered to have acted in the public interest if its total programming includes 4.75 percent news and 0.25 percent other public affairs broadcasts.[43]

A survey of eighty-six network affiliates in the top fifty markets, each with revenues over $5 million, indicated that the median figure for news and public affairs aired was 15.5 percent, more than three times the Commission's renewal standard.[44] While more encouraging than the results of the *Columbia Journalism Review* survey, the data do suggest that the Commission's renewal guidelines are too low and that many stations do not take their public affairs responsibilities seriously.

Important issues are raised when discussing the amount of time devoted to news and public affairs. Because television is a visual medium, it generally concentrates on those news stories that provide interesting and exciting pictures and film. Those stories, however, do not necessarily provide information important to the viewer. Many important stories, moreover, such as those on the economy, are given scant attention because they do not lend themselves to a visual presentation. Below Ron Powers gives some examples of news stories that provided minimal important information:

—at WLS-TV, the ABC-owned station in Chicago, there is a filmed report by the station's weatherman, John Coleman. Coleman is standing beside a highway in North Dakota. He holds an envelope toward the camera. He says, "In this envelope are a group of never-before-published pictures of flying saucers. Are these the real thing? Or . . . are these hoaxes?"

—at KNXT-TV, the CBS-owned station in Los Angeles, a woman reporter in a wet suit plunges into a tank of water. She begins playing with a porpoise.

—at KTTV, an independent television station in Los Angeles, co-anchormen Chuck Ashman and Charles Rowe are reading the night's lead stories. The lead stories include an item about a bill in the Tennessee legislature advocating a state fossil, and another item about a misprint in an *Azusa Herald* article announcing the appointment of Mary Hartman to the planning commission.

—at WMAL-TV in Washington, a woman reporter named Betsy Ashton is announcing a story on Howard Hughes' will. She is sitting in a cemetery.

—at KSTP-TV, the NBC affiliate in Minneapolis, comedienne Judy Carne pops into the newsroom during the newscast and begins playing with sportscaster Tom Rather's ears.

and finally,

—at WKYC-TV, the NBC-owned station in Cleveland, reporter Del Donahue is broadcasting from inside a lion's cage. The "angle" is that Donahue is "learning how" to train a lion. Donahue sits down upon the supine lion's haunches. The beast, which lacks a sense of humor, springs up and begins to maul Donahue, who suffers cuts requiring sixty stitches before he is pulled to safety by the real trainer. Journalism is served in the end, however: WKYC's camera records the entire grisly episode, and it is shown on several NBC stations—as a news event.[45]

This is also the era of the "news consultant," who packages the news to attract the largest audience. Often the television news staff responds to marketing priorities. "The on-air men and women look and sound less and less like their fellow citizens than like some idealized product of genetic breeding. This may be good for viewers' sexual fantasies; it does not do much for a station's credibility."[46]

While Powers may exaggerate, the quality of local news does vary greatly, and many station owners, who possess a lucrative government license, fail to adequately disseminate news and information on current issues to the public.

Ideally, the quality of news and public affairs programming would be improved because of public demand, not governmental. Chief Justice Charles Evans Hughes, writing the majority opinion in *Near v. Minnesota*,[47] claimed that a paper such as the *Saturday Press* "deserve[d] the severest condemnation in public opinion"[48] but that it cannot be silenced by an act of government. Modern broadcasting, however, seems largely free from criticism of its news and public affairs programming, save for a few academics and intellectuals who probably watch more public than commercial television. Moreover, news programs that concentrate most heavily on sensational rather than on informative stories often have the highest ratings in a given market,[49] which means that generally they have been very successful financially.

Besides the issue of the justification of federal regulation of broadcasting, the very real danger exists that the regulatory apparatus will be abused. During the Nixon administration, a concerted effort was made to harass broadcasters. Such tactics demonstrated not only the Nixon administration's hostility toward the media but also the particular susceptibility of broadcasting to such efforts. For example, when the administration found that the *Washington Post* was protected by the First Amendment, it attempted to intimidate it by challenging the renewal of the licenses of the *Post's* two Florida television stations. Two months after Nixon was reelected, in 1972, challenges to the stations were filed; one by a group headed by the chairman of the Finance Committee to Reelect the President, the other by a group that included two law partners of former Florida Democratic Senator George Smathers, the man who introduced the President to Bebe Rebozo. The White House had special reason to detest one of the *Post's* Florida stations; when G. Harrold Carswell was nominated for the Supreme Court, it was WJXT-TV in Jacksonville that exposed his pro-segregation record, which ultimately helped defeat him.[50] One tape revealed Nixon's animosity toward the *Post*:

> The [Washington] Post is going to have damnable, damnable problems out of this one. They have a television station . . . and they're going to have to get it renewed.[51]

Even though the challenges were unsuccessful, they did have an impact, for when filed with the FCC, the price of *Washington Post* stock on the American Stock Exchange dropped by almost 50 percent.[52] Moreover, whatever "self-censorship" was induced is impossible to measure. There has also been much speculation that Nixon made appointments to the FCC for the very purpose of punishing media owners that he found distasteful.

Other administration attempts at harassing the broadcast media were more direct. Charles Colson, special counsel to the President, was reported to have, over the telephone, threatened the presidents of the networks with sanctions if they did not change their coverage of White House activities. He allegedly said to Frank Stanton, then vice-chairman of CBS: "We'll bring you to your knees on Wall Street and on Madison Avenue."[53]

A Nixon legacy that haunted the networks for years was a series of Justice Department antitrust suits filed while John Mitchell was Attorney-General. The suits, filed against ABC,

NBC, and CBS, charged violations of antitrust laws in that the three networks determined who had access to network air time in such a way as to concentrate in themselves "ownership and control of television entertainment programs broadcast during prime-time evening hours."[54] While a number of the suits were quickly dismissed "without prejudice," a suit charging monopoly practices was only recently settled out of court by all three television networks.[55]

The Nixon administration, in order to influence news coverage, also tried to turn the affiliates against the networks. Clay Whitehead, then Director of the White House Office of Telecommunications Policy, in a speech delivered on December 18, 1972, proposed that *local* license renewal be contingent on certain network "behavior." In other words, the Nixon White House proposed to hold local stations responsible for the content of network news programming. If the Nixon administration could not change Walter Cronkite's news program, then the local affiliates who carried the program might. Although the networks themselves are not licensed, each network owns radio and television stations that are licensed, thereby making them vulnerable to administration pressure.

Finally, although not so ominous, former Vice-President Spiro Agnew stirred up public sentiment against the networks and charged them with bias. While discussion may be healthy, the Nixon administration was not interested in fostering reasoned debate; instead, it was interested in creating problems for the networks.

These examples raise the question of whether attempts to intimidate the broadcast media were unique to the Nixon administration or whether, in fact, the regulatory apparatus can at any time be used to influence news coverage. The question, unanswerable at this time, does indicate the extreme dangers that government regulation holds for broadcasting.

Partly because of the potential for government intimidation of the broadcasting industry and partly because of the damage done to the First Amendment, this chapter has not argued that there should be more government regulation; instead, it has argued that broadcasters should assume greater responsibility. A larger percentage of profits earned from a valuable government license should be spent on public affairs programming. One way to encourage this would be for the FCC to require that a minimum percentage of public affairs programming be aired. First Amendment barriers would most likely be cleared because such a rule would deal even less directly than the fairness doctrine with content. Unfortunately, the quality of public affairs programming, particularly those produced locally, would probably not improve. In addition, if broadcasters were required to provide a minimum percentage of public affairs programming, current budgets might be stretched to pay for the additional time, making public affairs even less interesting and informative. Considering the struggle over limiting the number of commercial minutes and the broadcasting industry's clout and access to other key actors in the FCC's political environment, it is questionable whether the Commission would even attempt such a plan, or even whether Congress would tolerate it. In addition, the courts would be severely limited in this area because they have largely left up to the Commission how individual licensees will fulfill their public interest responsibilities.

Many of the issues raised in this chapter are being considered as Congress attempts to "rewrite" the Communications Act of 1934. Much of the debate centers on the scope of regulation and considers altering or abolishing the fairness doctrine, personal attack and equal time rules, and other regulatory issues.

NOTES

1. *Broadcasting Yearbook*, 1980.
2. H.R. 13015 will be discussed in chapter 6.
3. Erwin G. Krasnow and Lawrence D. Longley, *The Politics of Broadcast Regulation* (New York: St. Martin's Press, 1978), p. 127.
4. Ibid., p. 130.
5. The same report authorized UHF as a supplement to VHF, but the Commission's report granted UHF second-class status.
6. Krasnow and Longley, p. 107.
7. Ibid., p. 112.
8. See chapter 3.
9. The decision also had the effect of putting a newspaper out of business. In March 1972, after all legal appeals had been exhausted, the Herald-Traveler Corporation was forced to relinquish control of the station, and a few

months later, the newspaper stopped publication, and its assets were sold to a competitor.

10. *Citizens Communications Center v. Federal Communications Commission*, 447 F.2d at 1210 (1971).

11. 326 U.S. 327 (1945).

12. *CCC v. FCC*, p. 1211.

13. Ibid.

14. Krasnow and Longley, p. 140.

15. "Picket Lines Due," *Broadcasting* (December 1, 1969): 10.

16. Krasnow and Longley, p. 143.

17. 24 F.C.C. 2d at 389 (1970).

18. "Analysis of FCC's 1970 Policy Statement on Competetive Hearings Involving Regular Renewal Applicants," Staff Study for the Special Subcommittee on Investigations of the House Committee on Interstate and Foreign Commerce, 91st Congress, 2nd Session (November 1970).

19. The staff study was not endorsed by members of the subcommittee or its chairman, Harley Staggers, who merely forwarded the document to the FCC with a request that the Commission submit a detailed legal opinion on the staff's conclusions. Krasnow and Longley, p. 147.

20. *CCC v. FCC*, p. 1206.

21. Ibid., p. 1208.

22. Ibid., p. 1214.

23. Norman Lear, Tandem Productions, remarks made at UCLA Communications Law Symposium, February 2, 1979.

24. Charles D. Ferris, "The Future of Television Networks," address delivered before the UCLA Communications Law Symposium, February 3, 1979, p. 4.

25. NBC reportedly spent well over $100,000 in legal expenses and thousands of hours in personnel time fighting the fairness complaint, which it eventually won. Steven J. Simmons, *The Fairness Doctrine and the Media* (Berkeley: University of California Press, 1978), p. 217.

26. Ibid., p. 226.

27. Ibid.

28. 376 U.S. 254 (1964).

29. Ibid., p. 270.

30. David Bazelon, chief judge of the U.S. Court of Appeals for the District of Columbia, remarks made at UCLA Communications Law Symposium, February 2, 1979. See also, "Bazelon, Ferris: More Sources of Programs Mean Less Regulation," *Broadcasting* (February 5, 1979): 29-30.

31. 438 U.S. at 748.

32. 418 U.S. at 258.

33. The increasingly complex libel laws have led some to doubt whether, in fact, the government has a "hands-off" approach to the print media.

34. Glen O. Robinson, *Communications for Tomorrow: Policy-Perspectives for the 1980's* (New York: Praeger Publishers, 1978), p. 441.

35. Mel Friedman, "A New Communications Act: The Debate Begins," *Columbia Journalism Review (September/October 1978): 41.*

36. *Lack of funding has always been a problem for public television. Remarks by Newton Minow, chairman, Public Broadcasting Service, at UCLA Communications Law Symposium, February 2, 1979.*

37. Ron Powers, *"Eyewitness News, (May/June, 1977): 22.*

38. *Broadcasting Yearbook*, p. B-47.

39. Ibid., p. B-33.

40. Ibid., p. B-36.

41. Ibid., p. B-49.

42. Simmons, p. 225.

43. Ibid.

44. Ibid.

45. Powers, pp. 17-18.

46. Ibid., p. 24.

47. 283 U.S. 697 (1931).

48. Ibid., p. 719.

49. The ABC-owned television stations in San Francisco and Los Angeles, which have specialized in this kind of format, in the past, have been at or near the top of the ratings for a number of years.

50. "Assault on the First," *Commonweal*, (February 2, 1973): 388.

51. Elizabeth Drew, *Washington Journal: The Events of 1973-1974* (New York: Random House, 1975), p. 277.

52. Carl Bernstein and Bob Woodward, *All the President's Men* (New York: Warner Books, Inc., 1974), p. 247.

53. Paul Laskin, "Shadowboxing with the Networks," *The Nation* (June 14, 1975): 715.

54. Ibid., p. 714.

55. The out-of-court settlement, agreed to by the last of the networks in September 1980, imposes a number of restrictions on networks in program ownership.

The Carter administration had also been active in this area. In July 1979, the Justice Department filed a suit in U.S. District Court in Washington, D.C., against the National Association of Broadcasters' Television Code, charging that it unfairly manipulates the marketplace by restricting the amount of advertising time available. The Justice Department claims the code violates antitrust laws. "Where Things Stand," *Broadcasting Magazine*, (September 1, 1980): 9.

6.
The Future of Broadcast Regulation

On June 7, 1978, the Communications Subcommittee of the House Committee on Interstate and Foreign Commerce released its draft of the "rewrite" of the Communications Act of 1934.[1] The chairman of the subcommittee and principal author of the rewrite, Lionel Van Deerlin (D-California), hoped that the House would pass H.R. 13015 by the end of 1979 and that it would be on the President's desk by the end of 1980.[2]

By January of 1981, however, Congress had abandoned any effort to pass a single, comprehensive rewrite of the Communications Act, and Congressman Van Deerlin, who said enactment of such a law would climax a long and satisfying career, was defeated for reelection in the Reagan landslide of November 1980.

In place of a single rewrite of the Act, the 97th Congress began considering a series of bills, each dealing with only a few issues. Those will be discussed below.

That the communications subcommittees of the 95th and 96th Congresses were unable to gain a consensus on a comprehensive rewrite is evidence of the ability of various actors in the regulatory environment to influence pending legislation. In the end, various groups and individuals were able to prevent the subcommittees from reporting out bills that would be approved by the full Houses.[3]

There is, nevertheless, much to be gained by discussing the original rewrite legislation. First, the provisions of H.R. 13015 which stirred so much controversy may be revived at any time as Congress considers various bills affecting regulation of broadcasting. Second, defeat of the effort to renovate the Communications Act demonstrated the relative strength of various actors interested in broadcast regulation. Such a "debate" provides an ideal forum for studying the political environment in which regulatory policy is formulated.

In addition, the bill offered many significant changes from the way broadcasting is currently regulated, and while those exact provisions may be tabled for the time being, the ideas suggested by them are not.

The most significant feature of H.R. 13015 was that it intentionally deleted the "public interest" standard used for nearly half a century and substituted a phrase that would provide for regulation only when market forces were not working: "The Congress hereby finds that the regulation of interstate and foreign telecommunications is necessary, to the extent marketplace forces are deficient."[4] Essentially, the bill made competition, not regulation, the focus of governmental oversight.

As H.R. 13015 was changed to accommodate a number of objections when the first draft was made public, it became known in some circles as "Rewrite II." The bill would have, among other things, freed cable television from federal regulation; allowed telephone companies to enter the cable field; virtually deregulate radio; lessen regulation of television; make the duration of broadcast licenses indefinite (immediately for radio, after ten years for television); and levy fees for use of the frequency.[5]

As expected, the user fee caused the most negative reaction among broadcasters. Rewrite II would have taxed the monopoly profits created by the FCC's allocation plan for television channels by levying a user fee based on the channel's worth as determined by its scarcity value.[6] Fees would be highest for network-owned stations and for the most profitable network affiliates. The money would go into a Telecommunications Fund, which would take in about $350 to $400 million annually. Of that sum, $50 million would pay for the new regulatory commission, replacing all congressional appropriations, $200 million for the development of public broadcasting programming, and $100 million to stimulate minority ownership of stations and to improve rural telecommunications.[7]

In July 1978 the subcommittee staff released figures that gave a clearer picture of how the contributions to the fund would break down. Under the working formula suggested by the subcommittee staff, a small commercial radio station would be expected to pay $200 to $800 yearly, while a high-powered, "clear-channel" operation would pay as much as $40,000.[8] The assessments for VHF television stations would generally begin in the six-figure range. In the New York metropolitan area, for example, which has the greatest number of viewing households in the country, each of the three networks' flagship stations fell into the $7 million bracket.[9] Broadcasters expressed concern that funding the Telecommunications Fund would be a permanent drain on station profits. National Association of Broadcasters Chairman Donald Thurston called it a tax: "In my view, any fee that reflects an amount beyond the cost of processing a broadcast license constitutes a tax on my business."[10] He objected to the fee as a "form of double liability" for broadcasters because the money would go "to finance competitive government programs" (public broadcasting).[11]

A number of provisions of H.R. 13015 had major First Amendment significance. One issue that was much debated was the substantial change made in the fairness doctrine. For radio stations, it would be abolished; for television, the Commission

shall by rule require television broadcasting station licensees to:

(1) provide news, public affairs, and locally produced programming (including news and public affairs)[12] throughout the broadcast day; and
(2) treat controversial issues of public importance in an equitable manner."[13]

H.R. 13015 would also have freed radio from equal time rules and free television from such rules in all national and statewide election campaigns.

Some proponents of deregulation, after arguing that fifty years of government regulation has produced blandness and timidity in programming, rejoiced in the change in the fairness doctrine. James Gabbert, president of the National Radio

Broadcasters Association, praised the plan as "the best thing that ever happened to radio."[14] The NAB, the largest lobbying organization, with over 5,000 member stations, was particularly concerned about the bill's separate treatment of radio and television and saw it as an attempt to divide broadcasters and dilute the influence of NAB's lobbying effort. Broadcasters were generally pleased with the repeal of the fairness doctrine and equal time rules, but many felt that the user fee was a high price to pay. Congressman Van Deerlin contended that the user tax and deregulation were part of a package and that the broadcasters could not have one without the other.

Citizen groups, some of which have long attempted to shape regulatory policy, were openly critical of the rewrite. The Reverend Everett C. Parker, director of the Office of Communications of the United Church of Christ, one of the oldest and most dedicated of such public interest groups,[15] denounced the rewrite as a "disgrace, amounting to a bigger giveaway of public rights and property than Teapot Dome."[16]

Public interest groups centered much of their criticism of the rewrite on the elimination of time-tested methods available under the Communications Act of 1934 and subsequent case law to challenge regulatory policy decisions, including the legal weapons of petition to deny license renewals, the fairness doctrine and equal time rules, and the FCC-sponsored initiatives promoting the equal employment of women and minorities. Under the rewrite, the "public trustee" concept would largely have been eliminated.

Some of the "pro-competition" provisions satisfied groups that blame many problems of broadcast regulation on the methods chosen by the FCC to allocate frequencies, particularly those of televivion. H.R. 13015 appeared to facilitate the growth of cable television and public broadcasting and to help make them stronger in relation to commercial radio and television. But the bill, as originally released, would lift only federal restrictions on the cable industry, leaving state and local authorities free to pass their own regulations.[17]

A major premise of H.R. 13015 was that the scarcity argument, long used to justify intense federal regulation, is no longer applicable to contemporary broadcasting. New technologies, most notably, cable television, satellite communications, "fiber optics," and low power television potentially increase the number of programs that can be received.

In *Red Lion*, the Supreme Court indicated that the scarcity argument lay at the heart of federal regulation:

> Where there are substantially more individuals who want to broadcast than there are frequencies to allocate, it is idle to posit an unabridgeable First Amendment right to broadcast comparable to the right of every individual to speak, write or publish.[18]

The rewrite tried to consider changing technological conditions and it made strides toward restoring the First Amendment rights of broadcast licensees. But by granting licenses indefinitely, the bill would largely have eliminated the comparative renewal process and would have made it even less likely that a challenger would be successful. In its original form, H.R. 13015 also weakened whatever marginal provisions currently grant citizens access to the airwaves.

Moreover, the bill may well have limited the diversity it sought to promote. The conditions by which others may enter the broadcasting field remain the same. The bill spoke eloquently of the "market," but in fact, a market may not actually exist, at least not in the sense suggested by the bill. Because of the monopoly situation currently enjoyed by established broadcasters, entering the field may not be financially feasible.

Although the bill cursorily recognized the First Amendment rights of broadcasters, it did not consider seriously the First Amendment rights of listeners and viewers. For example, because radio broadcasters are freed from the obligation to give fair coverage to controversial issues, those who own radio facilities because they got there first could broadcast their personal points of view and not provide access to those with differing opinions. Moreover, in cities where the only newspaper owns the only radio station, the impact on local elections, for example, could be significant. Under H.R. 13015, radio stations would have been under no obligation to serve the public interest or to present issues fairly.[19]

The "weight" of public opinion cannot prevent broadcasting

stations from acting irresponsibly. Because H.R. 13015 made it even more difficult and costly to challenge a license, station owners were likely to conclude that they can act with more independence. The public, despite technological advances, may not have access to many broadcasting signals and may hear relatively few opinions on local issues. The bill did not fully address the problem of integrating the new technology without limiting or ending access by nonbroadcasters.

After hearing major objections from public interest groups, subcommittee Chairman Van Deerlin agreed to make various changes in the original bill. In Rewrite II, he was hoping to win the support of a number of groups that had vowed to prevent passage of the legislation.

Public interest groups had voiced particular concern over deleting the public interest standard that has governed regulation of broadcasting for over half a century. While Van Deerlin reluctantly agreed to reinstate it, he repeated that the standard should not be used by "a majority of four out of seven commissioners to decide the will of Congress."[20] He warned that drafters of the bill "will spell out what we mean" by public interest.[21]

In addition, Van Deerlin responded to broadcaster complaints about the user tax and agreed to a percent limit on how much broadcasters would pay. The setting of the fees would be left to the Federal Communications Commission (restored in place of the Communications Regulatory Commission in Rewrite II), but under a ceiling established by Congress. The bill "should say something like not more than X% of revenues," Van Deerlin told a meeting of the Association of Independent Television Stations. But he refused to say what X would equal, saying only that "we have to keep in mind what is politically achievable."[22]

Cable broadcasters, while pleased that there would be significantly less federal regulation of their industry, were concerned that they were vulnerable to potentially crippling state and local regulations. Van Deerlin acknowledged that Congress may retain some control in the area to prevent such overregulation.

Van Deerlin also stated that he was flexible on the rewrite's provisions dealing with the fairness doctrine. While some viewed that section of the bill as enhancing broadcasters' First Amendment rights, Van Deerlin said that he was "not wedded" to requiring news and public affairs programming to be televised throughout the day. His intention, he said, was to prevent broadcasters from programming their public affairs shows during hours when fewer people are watching.[23]

Broadcasters, on the other hand, expressed much concern over the "throughout the day" requirement. NAB Television Board Chairman Thomas Bolger claimed that broadcasters are confused by the provision requiring stations to broadcast locally produced programming throughout the broadcast day. He asked:

Does this language mean that I must schedule a locally produced program once every hour or once every two hours? What should be the length of each program? Must I pre-empt the most popular prime-time network programs and insert a locally produced substitute? What will be the consequences if I fail to comply with this requirement?[24]

This provision attempted to maintain, at least to some degree, the concept of localism, which has been used to evaluate how well a licensee is serving the public interest, convenience, or necessity. But Bolger's comments represented substantial broadcaster hostility, and the provision was no more likely to provide locally produced public affairs programs than are the disastrous "prime-time" access rules currently requiring nonnetwork programming.

As Rewrite II was being debated on the House side of Capitol Hill, the chairman of the Senate communications subcommittee gave some indication of the future hurdles the bill would face.

Fundamentally, Senator Ernest Hollings (D-South Carolina) had reservations about "rewriting" the Communications Act of 1934, although he did agree that it needs "renovating." In a speech to the NAB regional conference in Atlanta in October 1978, Hollings said that broadcasters do not own the frequencies they occupy. He compared them to "ranchers who lease grazing rights on government land. And like the ranchers, broadcasters should pay for their 'grazing' rights." The Senator said, "not an unrealistic fee, but a fee nonetheless."[25]

In the same speech, Hollings neglected to discuss what broadcasters consider the other side of the coin, deregulation. Instead, he emphasized that broadcasters are public trustees and that they should continue to abide by such rules as equal time and the fairness doctrine.[26] He stated that a broadcast license should not be granted in perpetuity, comparing that to his own election to the Senate. It "doesn't mean since I got there first in 1966 . . . that I own it for the rest of my life. And since you've got that spectrum allocation . . . you don't own it for the rest of yours."[27] In broadcasting's favor, S. 611 (Hollings bill) would have lengthened television license terms from the present three years to five and would license radio stations indefinitely.[28]

The Hollings bill would also have answered broadcaster concerns raised by the U.S. Court of Appeals for the District of Columbia in the *WESH-TV* case. Under the bill, the FCC would have been prohibited from considering any other media interests of a renewal applicant in a comparative hearing, as long as the incumbent complied with FCC rules; it would also have prohibited consideration of management and ownership integration at renewal time.[29] Beyond those provisions, the Hollings bill would have left intact the entire system of broadcast regulation, including such procedures as comparative hearings and "ascertainment," the fairness doctrine, equal time rules, FCC-enforced Equal Employment Opportunity regulations, and the requirement that broadcasters serve the public interest, convenience, and necessity.

The Hollings bill would also have charged a user fee, which, although lower than that proposed by Van Deerlin, would generate $80 million annually, almost all of it coming from television broadcasters.[30]

As mentioned before, perhaps the most significant First Amendment issues raised in the rewrite dealt with the fairness doctrine and the equal time rules, whose relationship to government interference in programming requires they be examined in a First Amendment context.

The changes in the equal time provisions were not very substantial and may, in fact, have made the rules more workable. Some critics[31] claimed that they are impractical because they provide for equal time for opposing political candidates regardless of their level of support by the electorate.[32] Candidates of major parties and minor parties, independent candidates, and candidates in name only are entitled under the equal opportunity doctrine to equal broadcast time.[33]

H.R. 13015 would have rescinded the application of the fairness doctrine and equal time rules to radio stations,[34] and for television, it provided:

. . . if any television broadcasting station licensee permits any person who is a legally qualified candidate for public office to use any television broadcasting station operated by such licensee, then such licensee shall afford equal opportunities to all other such candidates for the office involved for the use of such station.[35]

The provisions of this section shall not apply in the case of candidates for the office of President, Vice-President, or Senate, or for any other office for which a statewide election is held.[36]

Section 439 carried forward the provision from the Communications Act of 1934 that prevents licensees from exercising control over the content or format of any material broadcast.[37] This section would also have continued to exempt coverage of a candidate during a newscast:

Any appearance by a legally qualified candidate for public office in any matter broadcast by a television broadcasting station licensee shall not be considered a use of the station involved within the meaning of this section by such candidate if such appearance occurs within the coverage of a news event.[38]

Section 439 further stated that its provisions impose no obligation on the part of the television licensee to allow use of the station by any legally qualified candidate for public office. While the current fairness doctrine requires stations to provide some coverage of election campaigns as part of their Part One responsibilities, the bill would have imposed no such obligation.

To some, this section was a vast improvement over the current law. While presidential candidates Jimmy Carter and Gerald Ford were able to debate on television during the 1976 campaign, they did so only because the courts refused to interfere with what the FCC had termed a bona-fide news event put on by a third party, the League of Women Voters.

If section 439 or something similar becomes law, it would probably allow more extensive debates to take place among candidates on the state and national levels, however, it did not clarify which candidates can be excluded from debates. The courts may still have to decide how substantial a candidate's support must be to enable him to appear with the major party candidates. It was also unclear about who is going to make the decision.

Of more First Amendment significance than the equal time rules was the substantial change in the licensee's fairness doctrine responsibilities. No longer would licensees have been obligated to make an affirmative effort to cover controversial issues of public importance, the often-forgotten Part One requirement of the current law.[39] The fairness doctrine would have been replaced with language that requires "equitable" treatment of controversial issues of public importance and the provision of news, public affairs, and locally produced programming throughout the broadcast day.

H.R. 13015 did not require that broadcasters affirmatively identify and cover issues of importance to their community. The potential abuses of radio and television licensees in local politics have been mentioned above. For both radio and television, the change in the fairness doctrine would have relieved broadcasters of much of their public interest responsibilities.

The Part One requirement, long-neglected by broadcasters, has rarely been invoked by the FCC. In the *Patsy Mink* case, a licensee did not broadcast any news related to strip mining, although the station's community was destined to be destroyed by it. Ordering the station to comply with the fairness doctrine, the FCC wrote, "a total failure to cover an issue of such extreme importance to the particular community would raise serious questions concerning whether the licensee had acted responsibly in fulfilling its obligations under the fairness doctrine."[40]

Some have argued for a quantitative formula that would require a minimum percentage of broadcast time to be devoted to news and public affairs.[41] Such proponents say that it does the least amount of harm to the First Amendment because it is significantly less content-oriented than the current fairness doctrine, which requires the Commission and the courts to second guess the editorial judgment of broadcasters. But section 434 of H.R. 13015, which was supposed to have the same goal as a quantitative requirement, actually did not. Section 434 would have eliminated the Part One requirement completely and would have required only that public affairs programming be broadcast throughout the day. It does not follow from its language that such programming will cover controversial issues of importance to the local community. Once again, the broadcasters' record with the prime-time access rule may indicate that public affairs programming may not actually cover important local issues.

The language of section 434 indicated that important members of Congress consider the Part One requirement of little use. They may be justified in their reasoning because it has been so infrequently invoked. Abandoning the requirement entirely, however, would undermine one of the major precepts of broadcast regulation and may more concentrate programming in the hands of the three networks and syndicated producers. The concept of localism, which Congress and the courts have reaffirmed in various forms, presumes that the broadcaster is best suited to ascertain the needs of his community and to broadcast issues of importance. This responsibility cannot be surrendered to the networks or to production companies that distribute syndicated programs. Even though a network affiliate may receive as much as 70 to 80 percent of its programming from the network, it cannot relinquish its Part One responsibilities to the network's headquarters so many miles from the community. In the past, community groups have insisted that local broadcasters listen to them and grant them access to their facilities. Moreover, local broadcasters have transmitted the feelings of their community to the networks. H.R. 13015 would not even have required broadcasters to identify their community's needs:

The Commission may not establish procedures to be followed by any broadcasting station licensee with regard to ascertaining the problems, needs, and interests of its service area.[42]

While H.R. 13015 did not totally repeal the fairness doctrine for television stations, it did substantially alter the concept of localism, which has been for fifty years a major tenet of broadcasting regulation.

Section 434 was the result of many years of unhappiness with the fairness doctrine as expressed by broadcasters and some First Amendment scholars. It has been argued recently that new technology and the lack of competition in the print industry make obsolete the distinction between print and broadcast media.

After H.R. 13015 was introduced and debated, and it became clear no single, comprehensive rewrite of the Communications Act would pass Congress, a number of bills were introduced by members of the communications subcommittees dealing with various aspects of broadcast regulation.

But in November, 1980, Republicans captured a majority of seats in the Senate for the first time in a quarter of a century. With the new Republican majority (and the defeat of some key Democrats in the House) came a new interest in deregulation. At the same time, Congress knew by January of 1981 that previous attempts to pass a comprehensive renovation of the almost fifty-year-old Communications Act were unsuccessful. Some of the bills introduced as the 97th Congress assembled in January, 1981, reflected previously discussed ideas, but many indicated the new interest in deregulation.

As the new chairman of the communications subcommittee, Senator Barry Goldwater's (R-Arizona) attitude about broadcast regulation cannot be taken lightly. In the 96th Congress, he and Senator Harrison Schmitt (R-New Mexico) introduced S. 622 that provided for a user fee to be collected from broadcasters, but one that would recover *only* the cost of regulation. S. 622 would have collected substantially less revenue than either H.R. 13015 or S. 611 introduced by Senator Hollings, then the communications subcommittee chairman.

As the 97th Congress began work, Goldwater introduced S.601. Applying only to television, the bill would:

—extend television licenses from three to five years;

—allow the FCC to grant renewal of a license after finding that 1) the licensee substantially met the needs of residents in its service area; 2) operation of the station has been free of any serious violations of the Communications Act or any FCC regulation; and 3) licensee continues to meet various character, technical, financial and other qualifications prescribed by the Communications Act.[43]

Among its most important provisions, S. 601 would prohibit the FCC from considering any competing applications for a license up for renewal. (This seems remarkably similar to S. 2004, considered but never passed by Congress). S. 601 would also allow the FCC to randomly choose among otherwise qualified applicants for a license. The Commission would have 180 days from enactment of the bill to establish a method.

Goldwater's bill contrasts in several ways with H.R. 1298,[44] introduced by Representative James Collins (R-Texas), ranking minority member of the House communications subcommittee. His bill would extend radio licenses from three to ten years, and television licenses from three to five years. H.R. 1298 would allow the FCC to substitute some other method for the comparative hearing process, but would prohibit the Commission from using auctions to choose among qualified applicants.

As with S. 601, H.R. 1298 would prevent the FCC from considering any competing applications for a license up for renewal until it had determined that the incumbent licensee had failed to meet the needs of its service area.

Not lost on current members of the committees was the provision of H.R. 13015 most hated by broadcasters. The new chairman of the Commerce Committee, Senator Robert Packwood (R-Oregon), introduced S. 821 that, besides placing a cap on appropriations for the FCC for the next several years, would institute a user fee for most providers of communications services; but Packwood's user fee would only cover half the cost of regulating the broadcasting industry. Congress would appropriate the rest.[45]

Finally, two bills dealing with the deregulation of radio, S. 270 introduced by Senator Schmitt and H.R. 1297, by Representative Collins, would eliminate the current requirement that radio broadcasters ascertain the problems, needs, and interests of residents in their service area.[46] The bills would also prohibit the FCC from regulating formats or requiring news, public affairs, or any other kind of programming. They would also make the license terms indefinite.

All of the above-mentioned bills may undergo significant changes as the various groups interested in broadcast regulation examine them. Some may not survive the legislative labyrinth that has proved fatal to other bills. But with the Republican majority in the Senate, and the mood in the country favoring deregulation, some of the bills face significantly brighter prospects in the 97th Congress than would have been true before the election. Whatever form the bills take, Congress must consider certain fundamental, constitutional issues as it prepares to change the way broadcasting is regulated.

Case law and legislation have largely supported the view that print and broadcast media are not equal before the Constitution. As discussed in chapter 2, the Supreme Court in *National Broadcasting Company v. United States*[47] held that the chain broadcasting rules were constitutional. The Court appeared also to be drawing a larger rule: that regulation in aid of free speech does not contravene freedom of speech or press. In the *NBC* case, Judge Learned Hand wrote for the three-judge trial court:

The Commission does, therefore, coerce their [the broadcasters] choice and their freedom and perhaps, if the public interest in whose name this was done were other than the interest in free speech itself, we should have a problem under the first amendment; we might have to say whether the interest protected, however vital, could stand against the constitutional right. But that is not the case. The interests which the [chain broadcasting] regulations seek to protect are the very interests which the first amendment itself protects, i.e., the interests, first of the "listeners", next of any licensees who may prefer to be freer of the "networks" than they are, and last, of any future competing networks.[48]

From the *NBC* case through *Red Lion*, the courts have maintained that diversity and access are goals of the First Amendment and that broadcasters may not ignore those who did not get a license.

It has been argued, however, and sometimes persuasively, that broadcasters are entitled to full First Amendment rights and that to deny them such rights does unnecessary damage to the vitality of the First Amendment's protections. A veteran television newsman, Bill Monroe, summed up his argument for full First Amendment rights this way:

Noble-sounding fairness and equal-time requirements that provide for government supervision of editorial decisions, penalize journalism that tackles controversial subjects, and discourage political debates.[49]

Monroe recommended that broadcast licenses be granted on the sole condition that stations adhere to their assigned frequencies.[50]

This argument, however, fails to consider the potential influence of broadcasters who promote their own viewpoints and candidates to the exclusion of those with opposing views. Moreover, this would likely lead to less emphasis on news and public affairs and to more emphasis on entertainment, which generates substantial revenues. Such a scenario, considering only the First Amendment rights of broadcasters, not those of the listeners and viewers, is extremely short sighted. It also translates the informing function of the First Amendment into a license to make money.

Many have argued recently that, because there are more than 10,000 radio and television stations and fewer than 2,000 daily newspapers, the scarcity argument is no longer accurate and does not justify a constitutional distinction between print and electronic media. Competition among daily newspapers in the same city, it is also argued, is almost a thing of the past. In view of such conditions, some have contended that the Supreme Court erred in the *Miami Herald v. Tornillo* case,[51] when it held unconstitutional a right-to-reply statute for newspapers. Those who question such a "double standard" maintain that any regulation of broadcasting beyond that concerning the technical aspects violates freedom of speech and of the press. Although conceding that the rules have not always been applied properly, this study has argued that sound distinctions can be made between the two media and that the fairness doctrine and the equal opportunity and personal attack rules are constitutionally permissible. Their misapplication is not sufficient reason for making newspapers and broadcasting constitutionally equal.

Broadcasting channels are owned by the people, while newspaper facilities are owned by the publishers. Still, Eric

Sevareid has some justification when he argues that such a distinction is irrelevant:

I have never understood the basic, legally governing concept of "the people's airways." So far as I know there is only the atmosphere and space. There can be no airway in any practical sense, until somebody accumulates the capital, know-how and enterprise to put a signal into the atmosphere and space. I have never understood why government should be empowered to affect the content of signals any more than it should affect the content of newspapers carried in the newspaper truck on the people's streets. I thought the traffic laws, in both cases, were enough.[52]

While Sevareid's comments may be appropriate for some levels of the broadcasting industry, it would be difficult merely to regulate the traffic of most radio and television stations and at the same time to keep licensees serious about fulfilling their public trustee responsibilities. Perhaps networks, with their national audiences and ability to attract the best broadcast journalists, are least in need of being reminded of their fairness responsibilities, including their obligation to cover significant issues. But local news organizations are not nearly so professional and are more likely to be associated with local political interests. In addition, networks do compete, in at least some respects, with national news magazines and with a handful of "national" newspapers. A broadcaster who owns the only television station in town (and may own the only newspaper also) is largely free to ignore his fairness responsibilities and may not receive a complaint from the FCC for years. Moreover, if he violates the Part One requirement of the fairness doctrine, he may never hear from the Commission.

Despite the persuasiveness of the lack-of-competition argument, such "impact rationale" is still less convincing than the responsibilities given the press under the First Amendment. The Framers singled out one institution in the Bill of Rights and provided it with special protection. But with such protection goes special responsibility. The First Amendment does more than just remove barriers to free speech and free press; it charges the press with the responsibility to provide information so that citizens can make intelligent decisions in choosing government officials and in shaping public policy. The First Amendment suggests that citizens have access to information that will enable them to keep their government accountable and responsible. If it is so narrowly construed as to apply only to the rights of broadcasters, and not to the rights of viewers and listeners, then the First Amendment will have become, in effect, a license to make substantial revenues and to exclude from the airwaves the opinions of those disagreeing with the licensee. At the core of the First Amendment, however, lie the concepts of diversity and access. The First Amendment protects those "silenced voices"[53] not fortunate enough to be granted a license, and Congress, the Supreme Court, and the Federal Communications Commission cannot ignore them.

The fairness doctrine indeed has been misapplied, and its abuse has unjustly injured the First Amendment claims of broadcasters. The *Pensions* case, discussed in chapter 3, is clearly one in which the Commission should have allowed NBC to determine how the documentary should have been "balanced." Despite the narrow margin of reversal, the U.S. Court of Appeals for the District of Columbia did prevent the Commission from stepping over the boundary and into the area of censorship.

It is also argued that the fairness doctrine and personal attack rules induce a form of "self-censorship" that is immeasurable but that deprives viewers and listeners of access to needed information. Even more than the fairness doctrine, the mass confusion that the Supreme Court has made of the libel laws[54] has done more to inhibit journalists, whether print or broadcast, than has the fairness doctrine. Because of the potentially huge damage suits and the Supreme Court's inability to formulate relatively clear rules, the libel laws provide a significantly greater threat to the First Amendment rights of all journalists than the fairness doctrine does to broadcasting. The Court's decisions in the area of "newsman's privilege"[55] and searches of newsrooms are more dangerous than its rulings on the First Amendment rights of broadcasters. A libel suit can wipe out and forever silence a newspaper or broadcasting station; but the Federal Communications Commission has been extremely reluctant to punish broadcasters for fairness doctrine violations. Despite the fact that the FCC annually *processes* several thousand fairness doctrine complaints against broadcasters, it takes action on relatively few of them.[56] In fiscal 1973, for example, the FCC received about 2,400 such complaints, but it forwarded only ninety-four of them to the broadcasters for comment.

Simmons, gathering statistics on fairness doctrine complaints for the years 1973-1976, found:

If the fiscal years 1973 through 1976 are combined, a total of 49,801 fairness complaints received by the Commission, resulted in 244 station inquiries (.406% of complaints), 54 adverse rulings (.108% of complaints), and 16 general fairness doctrine rulings (.0321% of complaints). In other terms, out of every 1,000 complaints received between FY's 1973 and 1976, approximately four resulted in station inquiries, one in adverse rulings, and '⅓ of 1' in a general fairness adverse ruling. The average complainant truly had only a 1 in a 1,000 chance.[57]

A basic difference exists between the purpose of newspapers and that of broadcasting stations. Despite newspapers' recent trend to provide nonnews entertainment items to bolster sales, newspapers are essentially conduits of news and information; that is their primary function, which is unaltered by the facts that it is purchased and that commercial advertisements are in its pages. Broadcasting stations, perhaps with the exception of all-news radio stations, are essentially media of entertainment, with news being a secondary function. Not to belittle the importance of television news, broadcasters, concerned with profit maximization, are less likely to go to great lengths to protect and promote the principles of the First Amendment, as was discussed in chapter 5.

Broadcasters should continue to press for the narrowest application of the fairness doctrine and personal attack rules and should vociferously complain when they are misapplied. Such conditions should allow broadcast journalism to flourish. This study has not argued that only "serious" broadcast journalism should qualify for First Amendment protection. If the Commission or the courts lean in that direction, broadcasters should vehemently protest.

Broadcasters have simply not shown sufficient devotion to protecting and promoting their First Amendment rights and responsibilities, particularly below the network level. Until programming that informs and educates is more prevalent, it would be inappropriate and premature to abolish the fairness doctrine. The courts must be ready to strike down excessive attempts on the part of the Commission to regulate the content of programming. But as long as the courts maintain jurisdiction in this area, broadcasters will need to go before them to have their First Amendment rights and responsibilities further defined. Although broadcasters do suffer under a ''second-rate'' First Amendment, to a large extent it is of their own making.

NOTES

1. H.R. 13015, 95th Congress, 2nd Session.

2. Ida Walters, ''Deciding TV's Future,'' *Inquiry Magazine* (February 5, 1979): 16.

3. H.R. 6121, introduced in December 1979, was approved by the House Commerce Committee in the summer of 1980. But the bill dealt only with common carrier provisions of the Communications Act of 1934 and did not involve the regulation of broadcasting.

S. 2827, which included broadcast provisions, ran into substantial opposition, and in late summer 1980, mark-up of the bill in the Senate Commerce Committee was postponed indefinitely.

4. Title I, section 101, p. 6.

5. In the original version of H.R. 13015, the Federal Communications Commission would be replaced by the Communications Regulatory Commission, to be composed of five commissioners instead of the present seven. A later version of H.R. 13015 known as ''Rewrite II'' restored the FCC with seven members as the agency charged with regulating the broadcasting industry.

6. The FCC's allocation plan for television, which was initiated in the 1940s, affects station profits in at least two ways. First, it protects them by limiting the number of competing broadcasting signals in an area. Second, the FCC's plan ties a station's prosperity to the number of homes its signal can reach because broadcast profits are derived from advertising revenues, which are based solely on the number of viewers a station's programming attracts. Walters, p. 17.

7. Section 413 of H.R. 13015. Mel Friedman, ''A New Communications Act: The Debate Begins,''*Columbia Journalism Review* (September/October 1978): 41.

8. Clear channel radio stations usually operate at 50,000 watts and are designed to reach remote areas of the country.

9. Friedman, p. 42

10. ''Broadcasting's turn in rewrite arena; NTIA weighs in on side of change,'' *Broadcasting Magazine* (September 11, 1978): 28.

11. Ibid.

12. The parentheses are in the bill.

13. Section 434 (a), H.R. 13015.

14. Friedman, p. 41.

15. The Office of Communications of the United Church of Christ brought the *WLBT-TV* case, which greatly expanded the standing of public interest groups in court. See chapter 3.

16. Friedman, p. 42.

17. In a later version, Van Deerlin said that Congress will provide some protection to the cable industry.

18. See chapter 3 for a discussion of the *Red Lion* case.

19. For an example of the potential abuses by radio stations, see the *WXUR* case in chapter 3.

20. "What's in store for Rewrite II?" *Broadcasting Magazine* (February 12, 1979): 36.

21. Ibid.

22. Ibid.

23. Ibid., p. 39.

24. *Broadcasting Magazine* (September 11, 1979): 29.

25. "Hollings takes tough stance on 'renovation,' endorses fees," *Broadcasting Magazine* (October 23, 1978): 23.

26. Ibid.

27. Ibid.

28. *Broadcasting Magazine* (March 19, 1979): 35.

29. Ibid.

30. Ibid.

31. Steven J. Simmons, *The Fairness Doctrine and the Media* (Berkeley: University of California Press, 1978), pp. 72-101.

32. Roscoe L. Barrow, "The Equal Opportunities and Fairness Doctrines in Broadcasting: Should They Be Retained?" *Comm/Ent* (San Fransisco: University of California, Hastings College of Law, vol. 1., Fall 1977): 79.

33. See chapter 1 for a discussion of the equal time requirement.

34. Friedman, p. 41.

35. Section 439 (a) (1) (A), H.R. 13015.

36. Ibid. (B)

37. Ibid. (B) (2).

38. Ibid. (C)

39. See chapter 1 for a discussion of the Part One requirement of the fairness doctrine.

40. Barrow, p. 95. 59 F.C.C. 2d 987 (1976).

41. Simmons, p. 225.

42. Section 434 (b), H.R. 13015.

43. "Legislative Scorecard on the 97th Congress," *Broadcasting Magazine* (April 13, 1981): 105.

44. Ibid.

45. Ibid.

46. Ibid., p. 106.

47. 319 U.S. 190 (1943).

48. 47 F. Supp. 940, 946 (S.D.N.Y. 1942).

49. Bill Monroe, "Unchain the Electronic Media," *Reason* (February 1979): 24.

50. Ibid., p. 25.

51. 418 U.S. 241 (1974).

52. Eric Severeid, "Why a Second-Class First Amendment for Broadcasting?" speech delivered on March 28, 1977, before the National Association of Broadcasters convention in Washington, D.C., p. 6.

53. "Bazelon, Ferris: more sources of programs mean less regulation," *Broadcasting Magazine* (February 5, 1979):29.

54. See *Time, Inc. v. Firestone*, 96 S. Ct. 958 (1976); *Gertz v. Welch*, 418 U.S. 323 (1974); and *Rosenbloom v. Metromedia*, 403 U.S. 29 (1971) in particular. The most recent libel cases began with *New York Times v. Sullivan*, 376 U.S. 254 (1964).

55. See *Branzburg v. Hayes*, 408 U.S. 665 (1972) and the Myron Farber case, 1978.

56. Barrow, p. 94.

57. Ibid.

Appendix: A "Systems" Model

Despite the considerable methodological problems involved, designing an analytical tool that evaluates how well the FCC regulates broadcasting in the public interest can be valuable. The selection of criteria for such evaluation must of necessity be subjective. It is impractical to measure the Commission's performance by the "public interest" standard alone inasmuch as the Communications Act of 1934 provides so few clues as to what constitutes the public interest, convenience, and necessity.

In this appendix, public interest will not be defined as a goal of regulation, although a working definition of public interest will be included. Instead, a "systems" approach will describe the relationship between the FCC and the actors in its environment. Considering the complexity of the FCC's political environment, constructing a model that measures empirically the relative importance of key actors in any policy or set of policy decision presents many problems. This approach does not assume that an examination of the *process* by which FCC policy is made will automatically reveal whether the goals of the organization are being fulfilled, namely, whether the public interest is being served. In fact, it is not assumed that the public interest will "emerge" from the bargaining process. The design chosen simply indicates that a "goal accomplishment" perspective presents serious methodological obstacles. Defining "public interest" precisely enough for use in such a model will have to wait further agreement as to what constitutes serving the public interest. As of now, serious disagreement over the meaning of public interest would render the model inoperative even before it highlighted important policy relationships. While the model does not look first to goals, it will be necessary to develop a working definition of the public interest as it pertains to the regulation of broadcasting.

To give the model focus and purpose, a set of questions has been developed. They will not be answered here, but they are the types of questions the model will be designed to consider:

1. Are the "interests" of the actors in the primary constituency (See chapter 4) more carefully considered and more frequently served than the interests of the secondary constituency?

2. Is the FCC, as are other regulatory agencies, guilty of over-identification with interest/clientele groups?

3. Is this overidentification with the regulated industries detrimental to the "public interest"?

4. Will an examination of FCC decisions over a period of months or years yield relatively clear patterns indicating the favoring of some interests and the undermining of others?

5. Is the "public interest" ever served by the clashing of other interests? Under what circumstances?

6. Does a sophisticated analysis of FCC policy decisions require the analyst to spend time on the premises of the Commission talking with policymakers?

7. Finally, are the data necessary to answer the above questions available? Can they be gathered?

In order to avoid an aimless search for purpose, the model requires a working definition of public interest. Admittedly, any definition will have a normative tint, but some attempt at defining the public interest is necessary. For purposes here, the "public interest, convenience, and necessity" will be assumed to have the following features:

1. In allocating frequencies, the spectrum will be divided in such a way that one station at a time will use a given channel or frequency and all parts of the country will be served by broadcasting stations. Furthermore, as technological advances allow, the spectrum will be expanded to allow greater access to the airwaves.

2. The FCC will provide opportunities for public participation in agency decision making.

3. Formal mechanisms will be constructed to consider input from public interest groups or lobbies even though such groups possess fewer resources than broadcasting lobbies.

4. The FCC will not serve the interests of the broadcasting industry to the detriment of the public interest.

5. The Commission will not unduly interfere with the programming and news decisions of broadcasters by imposing rules and regulations that have the result of dictating programming and news decisions.

6. Important FCC decisions will be announced publicly and will be widely reported in the general press.

While a number of the above issues are stated in general terms, the model will seek to identify, to the extent possible, the accomplishment of those goals in relation to the stated purposes of the Communications Act and the environment in which the FCC operates.

A number of features in the FCC's political environment make constructing a model particularly difficult. They need to be considered when designing it:

1. The policy and decision-making process of the Commission takes place over time. The Commission deals with a large number of issues, many of which are considered and acted on over a relatively long period of time. For example, Nicholas Johnson and John Dystel examined the operations of the FCC during a single day and concluded that it was forced to deal with many more issues than it could possibly handle.[1] During that one day, December 13, 1972, the Commission was presented with fifty-nine items. The authors concluded:

> The Commission lacks data, makes no independent analysis, relies heavily on information provided by interested parties, considers broad questions piecemeal, defers to industry interests, postpones difficult decisions, hopes for compromises that the agency can ratify, and fails to anticipate problems before they arise.[2]

2. FCC policymaking involves numerous actors located at many decision points. FCC policy is shaped, in varying degrees, by congressional committees, broadcasters and their lobbies, interested members of the general public, White House and other executive branch offices, and others. Any model that attempts to assign relative weights to the importance of those actors would have to be confined to relatively narrowly defined issues that would yield information about patterns of behavior among those actors.

3. The Commission deals with extremely complex issues. The regulation of the telephone and broadcasting industries requires expertise that may take years to acquire. As Johnson and Dystel suggest, the

commissioners are often uninformed about some of the issues that come before them. As with many organizations, the commissioners rely heavily on staff whose activities are less visible than their own.

4. As mentioned before, the goals of the organization are not clear.

5. Actors in the FCC's environment interact along formal *and* informal lines. While some formal relationships may have significant impact on FCC decisions and be easily described, more informal relationships, which may have important policymaking consequences, are more difficult to identify. Some method must be developed to uncover some of these informal relationships. Such informal relationships include:

a. Contacts between FCC/staff and members of Congress: a survey could be distributed to ask commissioners, staff, and key members of Congress how much contact there is among them, the nature of the communication, the purpose of the communication, and their perceptions of the effects of the communication on policymaking.

b. Contacts between FCC/staff and interest/clientele groups: a survey would ask lobbyists, such as those for the NAB, how much time is spent communicating with commissioners, staff, and others directly or indirectly involved in FCC policymaking.

c. Examination of trade press editorials: survey would ask actors in the FCC's political environment if they were influenced by editorial positions taken by the trade press.

d. Visibility of decisions, coverage in general media: examine amount of general interest and knowledge of FCC activities.

e. Public letters to or about FCC: examine letters to the editors of newspapers, letters to the Commission, letters to the public interest groups about Commission activities and policies.

TEST DATA FOR THE MODEL

By using policy issues that lend themselves to analysis to test the model, the analyst should be able to determine, to some extent, the circumstances under which certain actors influence policy decisions. The data themselves will not be gathered in this appendix. But issues will be identified that will highlight significant policy relationships among the actors in the FCC's environment. They include:

1. Appointment and service of commissioners.
2. Action on license renewals and challenges.
3. Decisions on expanding the spectrum.
4. Type of work after Commission service.
5. Court decisions.

6. Budget allocations.
7. Public participation in agency proceedings.
8. Lobbying by regulated and related industries.

The following data should be gathered:

1. Appointment and service of commissioners.
   a. identification and investigation
      —income and education of potential nominee;
      —job potential nominee currently holds;
      —industry sentiment on potential nominee;
      —congressional sentiment on potential nominee;
      —trade press attitudes on potential nominee;
   b. the decision to nominate
      —income and education of nominee;
      —job nominee currently holds;
      —industry sentiment on nominee;
      —expressed congressional sentiment on nominee;
      —trade press attitudes on nominee;
      —identification with regulated interests;
      —identification with members of Congress;
      —identification with nonregulated but related industries;
   c. the role of the Senate
      —committee vote on nominee;
      —floor vote on nominee;
      —number and percentage of nominees turned down by committee;
      —number and percentage of nominees turned down on floor;
      —number and percentage of nominees withdrawn by President;
      —number and percentage of nominees self-withdrawn;
      —description of obstacles to confirmation;
      —location of decision point where nomination ended;
      —number of times nominations ended at given decision points;
      —published description or criticism of nominee's philosophy;

2. Action on license renewals and challenges
   —number and percentage of licenses renewed without challenges;
   —number and percentage of licenses renewed with serious challenges;[3]
   —number and percentage of licenses renewed for less than three years with challenges;
   —number and percentage of licenses renewed for less than three years without challenges;
   —number and percentages of licenses not renewed with no challenges;

—number and percentage of licenses not renewed with serious
challenges;
—number and percentage of cases where company with larger
assets won license in comparative hearing process;[4]

This issue is extremely important to the model. One of the most
important functions performed by the Commission is the awarding of
licenses. The Commission in choosing licensees must consider whether
the grant of the license is in the public interest. But as Henry
Geller has written, the FCC "has shown a disposition to favor
existing licensees when it hears challenges from competing industry
interests, irrespective of whether the larger public interest is served."[5]
The information gathered for this issue would indicate the relatively
few times that the Commission has taken licenses away from established
broadcasting interests and has awarded them to others.

Much more data could be collected in this area, such as the
relative assets of companies awarded licenses during comparative
hearings, the amount of programming actually devoted to news and
public affairs compared with the promises made when the license was
awarded, and other related issues.

3. Decisions on expanding the spectrum
—number and percentage of decisions favoring expansion;
—number and percentage of decisions opposing expansion;

The data would indicate that the Commission, on a number of
occasions, voted to prevent expansion of the spectrum to protect
established broadcasting interests from increased competition.[6] The best
examples may be decisions affecting the development of UHF television
and the regulation of the cable industry.

4. Type of work after Commission service
—number and percentage of commissioners serving full term;
—number and percentage of commissioners serving partial term;
—average term;
—number and percentage of commissioners removed before
term expired;
—number and percentage of commissioners reappointed;
—number and percentage of commissioners not reappointed;
—description of subsequent career;
—number and percentage working for regulated interests;

—number and percentage working for nonregulated but related interests;

—number and percentage running for elective office;

—number and percentage serving in appointive office;

—number and percentage working for unrelated industry;

The charge that regulatory commissioners "cash-in" on their agency service after leaving needs to be investigated. An explanation as to why relatively few commissioners complete their full term is also necessary.

5. Court decisions
   —number of cases heard in federal courts relating to FCC;
   —number of cases decided in whole or part against the decision of the Commission;
   —number of cases sustaining FCC policy;
   —length of time necessary for FCC to carry out court decision;
   —number of appeals filed by FCC;
   —number of appeals filed against FCC;

The courts, as discussed in chapters 2 and 3, are an important part of the FCC's political environment. While court decisions usually follow Commission action on a particular issue, they do have an impact on future FCC policy.

6. Budget allocations
   —percentage of budget increase or decrease over several years;
   —instances of denial of special budget proposals;
   —changes made by OMB in budget;
   —changes made by congressional committees in budget;
   —changes made on the floor of Congress;
   —changes made by President or his staff;

Changes in the Commission's budget or denial of supplemental budget proposals may indicate congressional or White House discontent with FCC decisions. If denial of budget requests follows a particularly controversial decision by the Commission, the analyst may conclude that such action was related to the Commission's decision.

7. Public participation in agency proceedings
   —money spent by Commission to provide public access to

agency proceedings (transportation to and from Washington, for
example);
—number of times members of the public or public interest
groups have "participated" in agency proceedings.

8. Lobbying by regulated and related industries
—annual lobbying budget of NAB;
—annual lobbying budget of cable industries;
—annual lobbying budget of public interest groups;
—contributions to members of congressional communications
committees by regulated, nonregulated but related, and other
industries;
—money spent by industry for "entertaining" FCC commissioners
and members of the congressional communications committees;

It is difficult to determine the extent to which such "courting" by
interest groups influences FCC policy. Of course, commissioners
naturally are more likely to have contact with interested parties from
the regulated industries than with members of the general public.

CONCLUSIONS

Once the data have been gathered and the information compared with
the model of primary and secondary constituencies, relatively clear
patterns of behavior will begin to develop. For example, if one is
testing the hypothesis that the Commission is likely to favor established
broadcasting interests over other interests, including those of the general
public, information from issue areas 1, 2, and 3 will highlight such
a relationship. At this point, a theory could be developed suggesting
that when it comes to the appointment of commissioners, action on
license renewals, and expansion of the spectrum, the Commission
favors the interests of broadcasters and key members of Congress.
Then, looking back to the working definition of the public interest,
one could conclude that the public interest is not being served by
the appointment of commissioners closely identified with regulated
interests who make policy decisions that restrict competition in favor
of established broadcasters.

While these conclusions would be tentative and subject to modification
depending on certain conditions, they would allow the development of
theories that are empirically grounded as opposed to theories that
are based on casual observation. While theory development will depend to

some extent on the analyst's definition of the public interest, the model does allow the policy relationships to be identified and assessed regardless of one's definition of the public interest.

As mentioned before, the issue area that best highlights policy relationships is the appointment and service of commissioners. But an examination of commission decisions in the other issue areas would yield relatively clear patterns of decision making and would allow the development of theories relating to the role of various actors in shaping communications policy.

NOTES

1. Nicholas Johnson and John Jay Dystel, "A Day in the Life: The Federal Communications Commission," 82 *Yale Law Journal* (July 1973): 1575-1634.

2. Ibid., p. 1576.

3. Because some licenses are challenged by groups for publicity purposes or to influence license policy and not for the purpose of constructing and operating a broadcast station, some distinction must be made between serious attempts to take away licenses and attempts to influence policy.

4. The comparative hearing process is discussed in chapter 5.

5. Henry Geller, "A Modest Proposal for Modest Reform of the Federal Communications Commission," 63 *The Georgetown Law Journal* (February 1975): 707.

6. See chapter 5.

List of Cases

Abrams v. United States, 250 U.S. 616 (1919).

Ashbacker Radio Corporation v. Federal Communications Commission, 326 U.S. 327 (1945).

Brandywine-Main Line Radio v. Federal Communications Commission, 473 F.2d 16 (1972).

Branzburg v. Hayes, 408 U.S. 665 (1972).

Citizens Communications Center v. Federal Communications Commission, 447 F.2d 1210 (1971).

Columbia Broadcasting System v. United States, 316 U.S. 407 (1942).

E. G. Robinson v. Federal Communications Commission, 334 F.2d 534 (1964).

Farmers Educational & Cooperative Union of America v. WDAY, 360 U.S. 525 (1959).

Federal Communications Commission v. American Broadcasting Company, 347 U.S. 284 (1954).

Federal Communications Commission v. National Citizens Committee for Broadcasting, 76-1471.

Federal Communications Commission v. Pacifica Foundation, [438 U.S. 726 (1978)].

Federal Communications Commission v. Pottsville Broadcasting Company, 309 U.S. 134 (1940).

Federal Communications Commission v. RCA Communications, 346 U.S. 86 (1953).

Federal Communications Commission v. Sanders Brothers Radio Station, 309 U.S. 470 (1940).

Federal Communications Commission v. WOKO, 329 U.S. 223 (1946).

Federal Radio Commission v. Nelson Brothers, 289 U.S. 266 (1933).

Gertz v. Welch, 418 U.S. 323 (1974).

Gitlow v. New York, 268 U.S. 652 (1925).

Greater Boston Television Corporation v. Federal Communications Commission, 444 F.2d 841 (1970).

Bibliography

Aisenberg, Michael A., "Political Speech and the Electronic Soap Box: Citizen Access to Media in Post-Broadcasting America," 21 *St. Louis University Law Journal*, 1977.

"Analysis of FCC's 1970 Policy Statement on Competitive Hearings Involving Regular Renewal Applicants," Staff Study for the Special Subcommittee on Investigations of the House Committee on Interstate and Foreign Commerce, 91st Congress, 2nd Session (November 1970).

Ashmore, Harry S., "Broadcasting and the First Amendment: The Anatomy of a Constitutional Issue," *The Center Magazine* (May/June 1973).

"Assault on the First," *Commonweal* (February 2, 1973).

Bagdikian, Ben H., "Pensions: The FCC's Dangerous Decision Against NBC," *Columbia Journalism Review* (March/April 1974).

Barrow, Roscoe L., "The Equal Opportunities and Fairness Doctrines in Broadcasting: Should They Be Retained?" 1 *Comm/Ent* (San Francisco: University of California, Hastings College of Law, Fall 1977).

_____, "The Fairness Doctrine: A Double Standard for Electronic and Print Media," 26 *The Hastings Law Journal* (January 1975).

Bazelon, David, Chief Judge of the U.S. Court of Appeals for the District of Columbia, remarks made at the UCLA Communications Law Symposium (February 2, 1979).

_____, "FCC Regulation of the Telecommunications Press," *Duke Law Journal* (May, 1975).

Bazelon, Ferris, "More Sources of Programs Means Less Regulation," *Broadcasting Magazine.*" (February 5, 1979).

Bennett, William J., "Censorship for the Common Good," *The Public Interest* 52 (Summer 1978).

Berkman, Dave, "A Modest Proposal: Abolishing the FCC," 5 *Columbia Journalism Review* (Fall 1965).

Bernstein, Carl, and Woodward, Bob, *All the President's Men* (New York: Warner Books, Inc., 1974).

Bollinger, Lee C., "Freedom of the Press and Public Access: Toward a Theory of Partial Regulation of the Mass Media," 75 *Michigan Law Review* (November 1976).

Boyer, William W., *Bureaucracy on Trial: Policy-Making by Government Agencies* (Indianapolis: Bobbs-Merrill, 1964).

"Broadcasting's turn in rewrite arena; NTIA weighs in on side of change," *Broadcasting* (September 11, 1978).

Broadcasting Yearbook, 1980. Published yearly by *Broadcasting* magazine (Washington, D.C.).

Brown, Les, "Broadcast Regulation: Plan Makes Waves," *The New York Times* (June 12, 1978).

———, "Files Show the Nixon White House Tried to Mold Public TV Politically," *The New York Times* (February 24, 1979).

———, *Television: The Business Behind the Box* (New York: Harcourt Brace Jovanovich, 1971).

"Cable Television and Content Regulation: The FCC, the First Amendment and the Electronic Newspaper," 51 *New York Universtiy Law Review* (April 1976).

Canby, William C., Jr., "Programming in Response to the Community: The Broadcast Consumer and the First Amendment," 55 *Texas Law Review* (December 1976).

Cannon, Lou, *Reporting: An Inside View* (Sacramento: California Journal Press, 1977).

Canon, Bradley C., "Voting Behavior on the FCC," 13 *Midwest Journal* (November 1969).

"Charles Ferris—The Big Wheel at the FCC," *National Journal* (October 21, 1978).

Chase, Oscar G., "Public Broadcasting and the Problem of Government Influence: Towards a Legislative Solution," 9 *Michigan University Journal of Law Reform* (Fall 1975).

Cole, Barry, and Oettinger, Mal, "Covering the Politics of Broadcasting," 16 *Columbia Journalism Review* (November/December 1977).

Cronkite, Walter, "Privilege: Broadcast News and the First Amendment," 39 *Vital Speeches* (June 15, 1973).

Donaghue, Peter, "Reconsideration of Mandatory Public Access to the Print Media," 21 *St. Louis Law Journal* (1977).

Downs, Anthony, *Inside Bureaucracy* (Boston: Little, Brown and Company, 1967).

Drew, Elizabeth, "Is the FCC Dead," 220 *The Atlantic* (July 1967).

———, *Washington Journal: The Events of 1973-1974* (New York: Random House, 1975).

Emery, Walter B., *Broadcasting and Government: Responsibilities and Regulation* (East Lansing: Michigan State University Press, 1971).

"Federal Regulation of Television Broadcasting—Are the Prime Time Access Rule and the Family Viewing Hour in the Public Interest?" 29 *Rutgers Law Review* (Summer 1976).

Ferris, Charles D., "The Future of Television Networks," address delivered before the UCLA Communications Law Symposium (February 3, 1979).

Frank, Reuven, "A Fairness Doctrine of Journalists?" *The New York Times* (July 20, 1975), Letters to the Editor.

Freedman, Tracy, "Strange Bedfellows: Congressmen Who Own Media," *Washington Journalism Review* (September/October 1978).

Friedman, Mel, "A New Communications Act: The Debate Begins," 17 *Columbia Journalism Review* (September/October 1978).

Friendly, Fred W., *The Good Guys, the Bad Guys, and the First Amendment* (New York: Vintage Books, 1976).

_____, "What's Fair on the Air?" *New York Times Magazine* (March 30, 1975).

Geller, Henry, "A Modest Proposal for Modest Reform of the Federal Communications Commission," 63 *The Georgetown Law Journal* (February 1975).

_____, "The Comparative Renewal Process in Television: Problems and Suggested Solutions," 61 *Virginia Law Review* (April 1975).

"Geller's new, old design for distant signals," *Broadcasting Magazine* (February 19, 1979).

Gunther, Gerald, *Individual Rights in Constitutional Law* (Mineola, N.Y.; The Foundation Press, 1976).

Hilliard, David E., "Balance and Objectivity in Public Broadcasting: Fairer than Fair?" 61 *Virginia Law Review* (April 1975).

"Hollings takes tough stance on 'renovation,' endorses fees," *Broadcasting Magazine* (October 23, 1978).

Johnson, Nicholas, "A New Fidelity to the Regulatory Ideal," 59 *The Georgetown Law Journal* (March 1971).

_____, *How to Talk Back to Your Television Set* (Boston: Little, Brown and Company, 1967).

_____, and Dystel, John Jay, "A Day in the Life: The Federal Communications Commission," 82 *Yale Law Journal* (July 1973).

Kahn, Frank J., *Documents of American Broadcasting*, 2nd ed. (Englewood Cliffs, N.J.: Prentice-Hall Inc., 1973).

Kalven, Harry Jr., "Broadcasting, Public Policy and the First Amendment," 10 *The Journal of Law and Economics* (October 1967).

Knoll, Steve, "Fair or Foul?" *The New Republic* (August 31, 1974).

Krasnow, Erwin G., and Longley, Lawrence D., *The Politics of Broadcast Regulation* (New York: St. Martin's Press, 1978).

Lane, James M., "Constitutional Law—*Pacifica Foundation v. FCC:* First Amendment Limitations on FCC Regulation of Offensive Broadcasts," 56 *North Carolina Law Review* (April 1978).

Lange, David L., "The Role of the Access Doctrine in the Regulation of the Mass Media: A Critical Review and Assessment," 52 *North Carolina Law Review* (November 1973).

Laskin, Paul, "Shadowboxing with the Networks," *The Nation* (June 14, 1975).

Lear, Norman, Tandem Productions, remarks made at the UCLA Communications Law Symposium (February 2, 1979).

Lee, Robert E., "The FCC and Regulatory Duplication: A Case of Overkill?" 51 *Notre Dame Lawyer* (December 1975).

Lichty, Lawrence, "Members of the Federal Radio Commission and Federal

Communications Commission: 1927-1961," 6 *Journal of Broadcasting* (Winter 1961-1962).

Lipsky, Abbott B., Jr., "Reconciling *Red Lion* and *Tornillo:* A Consistent Theory of Media Regulation," 28 *Stanford Law Review* (February 1976).

Loevinger, Lee, "Is There Intelligent Life in Washington?" 29 *Federal Communications Bar Journal* (1976).

McKay, Robert B., "National News Council as National Ombudsman," 21 *St. Louis University Law Journal* (1977).

MacNeil, Robert, *The People Machine: The Influence of Television on American Politics* (New York: Harper & Row, 1968).

Maeder, Gary William, "Right of Access to the Broadcast Media for Paid Editorial Advertising—A Plea to Congress," *UCLA Law Review* (October 1974).

Millard, Steve, "Broadcasting's Pre-Emptive Court," *Broadcasting Magazine* (August 30, 1971).

Miller, Jonathan, "HR 13015: The Battle Lines Are Drawn," *TV Guide* (September 23, 1978).

Minow, Newton, chairman, Public Broadcasting Service, remarks made at the UCLA Communications Law Symposium (February 2, 1979).

———, *Equal Time: The Private Broadcaster and the Public Interest* (New York: Atheneum, 1964).

"Minow Observes a 'Vast Wasteland,' " *Broadcasting Magazine* (May 15, 1960).

Monroe, Bill, "Unchain the Electronic Media," *Reason* (February 1979).

Mosher, Frederick C., *Basic Documents of American Public Administration, 1776-1950* (New York: Holmes & Meier Publishers, Inc., 1976).

Nelson, Harold L., and Teeter, Dwight L., Jr., *Law of Mass Communications: Freedom and Control of Print and Broadcast Media* (Mineola: The Foundation Press, Inc., 1969).

Phillips, Wayne, "Jamming the Fairness Doctrine," *The Nation* (May 3, 1975).

"Picket Lines Due," *Broadcasting Magazine* (December 1, 1969).

"The Pool of Experts on Access," *Broadcasting* (September 20, 1971).

Powers, Ron, "Eyewitless News," 16 *Columbia Journalism Review* (May/June 1977).

Prager, Eileen Carroll, "Public Figures, Private Figures and the Public Interest," 30 *Stanford Law Review* (November 1977).

"Press Protections for Broadcasters: The Radio Format Change Cases Revisited," 52 *New York University Law Review* (May 1977).

Price, Monroe E., "The First Amendment and Television Broadcasting by Satellite," 23 *UCLA Law Review* (June 1976).

Pritchett, C. Herman, *The Roosevelt Court* (Chicago: Quadrangle Books, 1948).

"The Regulation of Competing First Amendment Rights: A New Fairness Doctrine Balance After *CBS?*" 122 *University of Pennsylvania Law Review* (May 1974).

Robinson, Glen O., ed., "The Judicial Role," *Communications for Tomorrow: Policy Perspectives for the 1980's* (New York: Praeger Publishers, 1978).

Roper Survey, 1976, 1978, 1980.

"Senate Beats Van Deerlin to the Draw on 1934 Law," *Broadcasting Magazine* (March 19, 1979).

Sevareid, Eric, "Why a Second-Class First Amendment for Broadcasting," speech delivered on March 28, 1977, before National Association of Broadcasters convention in Washington D.C.

Shaw, David, "Newspapers Challenged as Never Before," *Los Angeles Times* (November 26, 1976).

Simmons, Steven J., *The Fairness Doctrine and the Media* (Berkeley: University of California Press, 1978).

———, "Fairness Doctrine: The Early History," 29 *The Federal Communications Bar Journal* (1976).

———, "The FCC's Personal Attack and Political Editorial Rules Reconsidered," 125 *University of Pennsylvania Law Review* (May 1977).

Smith, Jerome R., "Telecommunications—The FCC's Fairness Doctrine Not Applied to Advertisements for Commercial Products," 25 *Emory Law Journal* (Spring 1976).

Sundermeyer, Michael S., "Filthy Words, the FCC, and the First Amendment: Regulating Broadcast Obscenity," 61 *Virginia Law Review* (April 1975).

Thorp, Bruce, "Washington Pressures/Radio-TV lobby fights losing battle against rising federal control." *National Journal* (August 22, 1970).

United States Senate, Committee on Commerce, "Agency Comments on the Payment of Reasonable Fees for Public Participation in Agency Proceedings" (January 1977).

———, "Appointments to the Regulatory Agencies: The Federal Communications Commission and the Federal Trade Commission (1949-1974)," (April 1976).

———, "Oversight of the Federal Communications Commission" (April 21 and 22, 1975).

Wade, John W., "The Communicative Torts and the First Amendment," 48 *Mississippi Law Journal* (September 1977).

Walters, Ida, "Deciding TV's Future," *Inquiry Magazine* (February 5, 1979).

"What's in Store for Rewrite II?" *Broadcasting Magazine* (February 12, 1979).

"Where Things Stand," *Broadcasting Magazine* (February 5, 1979).

Whitehead, Clay T., "Broadcasters and the Network: The Responsibility of the Local Station," 39 *Vital Speeches* (February 1, 1973).

Wicker, Tom, *On Press* (New York: The Viking Press, 1978).

Wiley, Richard E., "Communications Law: Policy and Problems," 61 *Virginia Law Review* (April 1975).

Williams, Wenmouth, Jr., "Impact of Commissioner Background on FCC Decisions: 1962-1975," 20 *Journal of Broadcasting* (Spring 1976).

Wilson, Gray W., "Right of Access to Broadcasting: The Supreme Court Takes a Dim View," 62 *The Georgetown Law Journal* (October 1973).

Wise, D. Scott, "Growing Deference to the Broadcaster's First Amendment Rights," *1976 Annual Survey of American Law*, New York University School of Law (1977).

Zeidenberg, Leonard, "Moving More Muscle into Washington," *Broadcasting Magazine* (February 21, 1972).

———, "The Struggle Over Broadcast Access II," *Broadcasting Magazine* (September 27, 1971).

Index

ABOUT THE AUTHOR

Richard E. Labunski is both a political scientist specializing in First Amendment law and a veteran broadcast journalist. He has taught political science at the University of California, Santa Barbara where he received his Ph.D. and at the University of Nevada, Reno. He also has ten years of news experience in radio and television, including work in New York, San Francisco, Washington, D.C., Tucson, and Reno. He has worked as a general assignment, consumer, and investigative reporter.